My Father's War

My Father's War

Confronting Norway's Nazi Past

Bjørn Westlie

Translated by Dean Krouk

THE UNIVERSITY OF WISCONSIN PRESS

Publication of this book has been made possible, in part, through support from the Anonymous Fund of the College of Letters and Science at the University of Wisconsin–Madison. This production has been published with the financial support of NORLA.

The University of Wisconsin Press
728 State Street, Suite 443
Madison, Wisconsin 53706
uwpress.wisc.edu

Gray's Inn House, 127 Clerkenwell Road
London ECIR 5DB, United Kingdom
eurospanbookstore.com

Library of Congress Cataloging-in-Publication Data

Names: Westlie, Bjørn, author. | Krouk, Dean, translator.
Title: My father's war : confronting Norway's Nazi past /
Bjørn Westlie ; translated by Dean Krouk.
Other titles: Fars krig. English
Description: Madison, Wisconsin : The University of Wisconsin Press, [2023] |
Originally published by H. Aschehoug & Co. under the title Fars Krig,
copyright ©2008 by H. Aschehoug & Co. (W. Nygaard), Oslo. |
Includes bibliographical references.
Identifiers: LCCN 2022039132 | ISBN 9780299343248 (hardcover)
Subjects: LCSH: Westlie, Petter, 1919- | Waffen-SS—History. |
Soldiers—Norway—Biography. | World War, 1939–1945—Collaborationists—Norway. |
World War, 1939–1945—Campaigns—Soviet Union.
Classification: LCC D757.85 .W4713 2023 | DDC 940.54/1343—DC23/eng/20221024
LC record available at https://lccn.loc.gov/2022039132

To my
granddaughter
ALVA

To us, their descendants, who are not historians and are not carried away by the process of research and can therefore regard the event with unclouded common sense, an incalculable number of causes present themselves. The deeper we delve in search of these causes the more of them we find; and each separate cause or whole series of causes appears to us equally valid in itself and equally false by its insignificance compared to the magnitude of the events, and by its impotence—apart from the cooperation of all the other coincident causes—to occasion the event.

—LEO TOLSTOY, *War and Peace*

Contents

Translator's Introduction

Why would someone from Nazi-occupied Norway volunteer as a soldier on the German side in World War II, supporting the regime that had invaded in April 1940 and would occupy the country for the next five years? What were the motivations of the *frontkjempere*, to use the Norwegian term for these volunteer "front fighters," many of whom served on the eastern front? Both during the war and in the postwar decades, they were treated as traitors and disgraces to the nation in Norway as in other occupied countries. One of them was Petter Westlie, the father of the journalist and historian Bjørn Westlie. As a young man, Petter was so zealous in his support for Nazi Germany that he changed the spelling of his surname, Vestli, to make it look more German.

This remarkable book, first published in Norwegian as *Fars krig* in 2008, received the prestigious Brage Prize for best work of nonfiction. It tells the story of Petter's time as a volunteer soldier in the Waffen-SS, including how he ended up as a volunteer soldier and what it meant for his life afterward. This story covers not only collaboration and treason in occupied Norway but also the German invasion of the Soviet Union in 1941–42 and the atrocities committed against Ukrainian Jews during the Holocaust. Combining his own family letters and records, including tape recordings from his father, with careful historical research, Westlie attempts to fill in the silences and gaps in the family's knowledge of Petter's past, to discover the truth about what his father did in Norway and Ukraine during the war.

Before he wrote this book, Westlie was already a significant voice in Norwegian public discourse about World War II and the Holocaust. In the 1990s, he published articles in the newspaper *Dagens Næringsliv* that reported on the confiscation of Jewish property during the occupation. This reporting led to the establishment of a government commission that resulted in compensation for the Jewish population in Norway as well as the establishment of the Norwegian Center for Holocaust and Minority Studies. In 2002, Westlie published the important book *Oppgjør i skyggen av Holocaust* (Reckoning in the shadow of the Holocaust), which recounts these historical events and the process of restitution. Since then, he has published several other books on topics such as the spread of antisemitic propaganda in the nazified Norwegian press during the war.

As a *frontkjemper*, Petter Westlie was a member of the SS Division Wiking. This division was not part of the Wehrmacht (the German armed forces from 1935 to 1945) but rather the military wing of the SS, known as the Waffen-SS. Led by Heinrich Himmler, the SS was the major paramilitary organization in Nazi Germany and was responsible for the regime's racial policy. As a northern nation whose inhabitants were idealized in Nazi racial doctrines, Norway figured largely in Nazi leaders' vision of a future Germanic empire.[1] Although most Norwegians did not share this vision, some young men volunteered to fight for Germany and defend their ideal of European civilization from the multiple threats they saw in Soviet Bolshevism, English liberalism, and "international Jewry." Such "Germanic" volunteers numbered in the tens of thousands and came not only from Norway but Sweden, Denmark, the Netherlands, Switzerland, and other regions that were part of the alleged racial brotherhood.[2]

The total number of Norwegians who served on the German side during the war was around 4,500, and most of them were in various Waffen-SS divisions.[3] Around 850 of these Norwegian *frontkjempere* had died by May 1945, while many others who had survived had lasting injuries and were sentenced to serve time in prison or labor camps in postwar Norway after the legal purge of collaborators.[4] Many of these men had a right-wing extremist background, and the racist and ideological elements of the Waffen-SS reinforced their reactionary Norwegian nationalism. Research has shown that although many of the front soldiers supported a nazified Norway, they did not necessarily support the integration of Norway into a greater Germanic Reich.[5]

The relationship between the Norwegian fascist party, Nasjonal Samling (NS), and the SS in Norway was likewise defined by a split between

Norwegian fascist nationalism and pan-Germanic Nazism. NS was founded by Vidkun Quisling as an extremist nationalist and anticommunist party in 1933. It was never a significant or popular party at a national level in the 1930s, and it won only 1.8 percent of the vote in 1936, the last federal election before the outbreak of World War II.[6] And yet several months after the invasion of Norway, NS was made the only legal party in the country. Despite this, only twenty-five thousand Norwegians had become party members by the start of 1941. An estimated fifty to sixty thousand Norwegians were members of NS at some point during the war (less than 0.02 percent of the 1940 population of nearly three million).[7]

After the liberation, the Norwegian fascists and collaborators became pariahs, a source of shame and anger in the collective memory of the period. In the late 1990s, a Norwegian historian noted that the topic of the *frontkjempere* was taboo, an aspect of Norwegian war history that inspired *berørings-angst* (an anxiety about touching on a sensitive topic).[8] That is no longer the case. In the twenty-first century, volunteer soldiers have been the subject of much historical research and debate, though they can still inspire public controversy, as the Norwegian Broadcasting Company's documentary series *Frontkjempere* (2021) did.[9] Similarly, the Norwegian Holocaust and the history of antisemitism in Norway have received renewed attention in the twenty-first century and especially since 2012, the year of the Norwegian state's official apology for its complicity in deporting Jews during the occupation. Since then, major historical works on the topic have been published, including Bjarte Bruland's 2017 *Holocaust i Norge* (The Holocaust in Norway). While the events of the Holocaust in Norway have been known for decades, they have not always been as central to the public memory and understanding of the war era as they have become in recent decades.

My Father's War remains a signal contribution to this literature. It is a brave work of nonfiction that goes to the heart of a nationally sensitive topic and that discloses an agonizing family history. In prose that is sober and plain but also reflective and tense, Westlie reconstructs his father's story from the interwar years to his participation in Operation Barbarossa in 1941 to the early twenty-first century, when the ideological cold war that characterizes the relationship between father and son starts to thaw. The implicit question of when the attempt to understand the motives of a pro-Nazi volunteer soldier, even for a son seeking to comprehend his distant father, becomes *too sympathetic* is ever present. A large part of what makes the book successful is the balance it strikes between the desire for understanding and the refusal to excuse. Westlie provides the reader with great insight into the context in which his father made his choices and into his motivations, and yet he never abandons the role of a critical historian and investigative reporter. In the end, *My Father's War* is also about the postwar aftermath of Petter's decision to sacrifice his youth to a political cult and about the complex legacies of ethnonationalism in contemporary Norway. For readers interested in the long shadows of the twentieth century in contemporary life, Westlie's book is a riveting experience.

RECOMMENDED READING IN ENGLISH

Gilmour, John, and Jill Stephenson, eds. *Hitler's Scandinavian Legacy.* London: Bloomsbury, 2013.

Gutmann, Martin R. *Building a Nazi Europe: The SS's Germanic Volunteers.* Cambridge: Cambridge University Press, 2017.

Hassing, Arne. *Church Resistance to Nazism in Norway, 1940–1945.* Seattle: University of Washington Press, 2014.

Maier, Ruth. *Ruth Maier's Diary: A Young Girl's Life under Nazism.* Edited by Jan Erik Vold. Translated by Jamie Bulloch. New York: Vintage Books USA, 2010.

Österberg, Mirja Johan Östling, and Henrik Stenius, eds. *Nordic Narratives of the Second World War: National Historiographies Revisited.* Lund: Nordic Academic Press, 2011.

Søbye, Espen. *Kathe—Always Been in Norway.* Translated by Kerri Pierce. Oslo: Krakiel, 2019.

Stecher-Hansen, Marianne, ed. *Nordic War Stories: World War II as History, Fiction, Media, and Memory.* New York: Berghahn, 2021.

Stratigakos, Despina. *Hitler's Northern Utopia: Building the New Order in Occupied Norway.* Princeton, NJ: Princeton University Press, 2022.

My Father's War

Prologue

The Little Wooden Box from Ukraine

I was never close to my father when I was growing up in the 1950s and 1960s. I didn't dare to get closer to him because I was afraid of touching on the "unmentionable." Something was hidden inside him, and I didn't want to know about it. As a young teenager, I was already aware that we couldn't discuss the war or Nazism. It was best to leave things unsaid.

The distance between us only grew when I embraced political views that were the exact opposite of his. Things didn't improve when he found out that my best friend's father had spent several years in German POW camps and that my first father-in-law had been imprisoned by the Germans during the occupation of Norway. I guess it wasn't so strange that my father felt left out in the cold. And yet I think we both wanted to be closer.

Up until 1992, our relationship took the form of a tacit agreement to avoid discussing anything but superficial matters. But as his opposition to immigration grew more and more pronounced, the result was a confrontation and a falling out. When he learned that the curriculum for my daughter's civil confirmation included an introduction to Islam, he lost it. Islam was, for him, the greatest threat to us Norwegians. I couldn't help connecting his fear of Muslims to an even more unpleasant topic.

"Haven't you learned anything at all?" I asked.

It was the most hurtful thing I could have said to him. At that point, I didn't realize that I was the stronger one in our relationship.

Our falling out lasted for a long time; we had no contact for four years. The fact that I wouldn't listen to him and turned away made him even more lonely, dejected, and bitter. He had a son who had chosen the wrong side, a son who belonged to the enemy camp. In those years I too thought of

3

him as an enemy. I tried to forget him. Perhaps that was the easiest thing to do. It relieved me of responsibility.

～

At home in his tiny apartment, my father amassed large piles of newspaper clippings, on which he wrote comments by hand. Much of it had to do with immigrants and politics—and World War II. He was alone, with no one to talk to, so he talked to himself using a simple tape recorder. A tall stack of cassettes gradually formed as he continued to mull over the same issues from his past.

He was the one, not me, who finally reached out. In 1996, he sent me a letter and a cassette. It was something of an attempt at a reconciliation. On the recording, I heard:

> Your angry outbursts are still hanging in the air, which bothers me—as do my outbursts. I sometimes think, when I'm having these conversations with myself, that it's always possible to call a family member on the phone. But I'm afraid it will lead nowhere, and that you'll turn your back on me again. You'd probably just hang up. Not that there's any guarantee that you're listening now—maybe you'll just ignore me completely. But try and make an exception. You can at least spend a bit more time on me, even if it's only out of curiosity. I've certainly spent a lot of time trying to understand you. Maybe we won't be any closer after this—but I hope we don't grow any farther apart. We are certainly far apart when it comes to how we see the country's political leadership.

My father also said that he didn't think "either of us wishes the other any harm" but that there would always be subjects we would need to avoid: "Our lives could probably continue with the four or five meetings a year, when we wouldn't talk about anything difficult, out of fear or perhaps cowardice. We would talk about the weather and the wind, like strangers meeting in the park."

I remained unable to accept my father's request for contact. On a card I sent him in May 1996, I wrote: "I am writing now so that you'll understand that I haven't forgotten you, so you won't think that the letter and the cassette you sent meant nothing to me. I just need time to let it all sink in and to prepare an answer for you."

But there was no answer from me—not then.

~

Another year would pass before we were in touch again, this time on the telephone. A few superficial words about how things were going—"Yeah, things have been alright"—but nothing more. Then, one day in the autumn of 1997, I ran into him by chance at Youngstorget, a square in downtown Oslo. We said hello and exchanged a few words, but then it ground to a halt again. I was locked inside myself, and neither of us managed to break through.

Some years passed, and we talked on the telephone from time to time.

In 2003, he wanted to give me more cassette recordings he had made for me. They were in a shoebox, which my daughter went and picked up. She earnestly wished for me and my father to get along better and was hurt by the whole situation. She wanted him to be her grandfather.

I listened to some of the recordings before setting them aside. They were letters to me in his voice, and it was all too difficult. He told me about certain parts of his life story, about his youth in the 1930s, the outbreak of war and his time as a volunteer soldier in the SS during the German invasion of Ukraine in 1941. But also about his disappointments, betrayals, and feelings of despair.

The shoebox stayed in a plastic bag in the closet for a long time. Then one day, I took it out and started to listen, hour by hour. Slowly, I began to see my father in a new light. I started to dream about him—and tried to imagine what his life was like.

~

I imagine my father in the autumn of 1998, as he tries to hurry across Torggata, the street with all the kebab shops he despises. His small apartment is in a backyard building behind address number 32. It is drafty and cold in the winter and quite miserable. He is surrounded by people he refers to as "foreigners," and he only leaves the house when he needs to go shopping. It is always crowded in the stretch of the street between Torggata

Baths and St. James's Church, and my father feels as if he is being pushed off the sidewalk by groups of young immigrants who don't give him any room to pass. It feels threatening to him, but he has an important errand. He crosses Youngstorget, walks through the Opera passage, and continues to the corner of Storgata, where Berntzen's Bookshop is located.

He eagerly pays 329 kroner for the book he has ordered from Denmark. He has been waiting for *Under the Swastika and the Danish Flag* [*Under hagekors og Dannebrog*], which deals with the Danish volunteer soldiers in the Waffen-SS in the years 1940–45. The authors, Danish historians, write about the Waffen-SS and Regiment Nordland, the division my father was in. He must have read or heard from someone that this book was critical of the Danish volunteers on the eastern front—and thus also the ones from Norway. It is the first serious historical examination of what the Nordic volunteers were doing during Nazi Germany's Operation Barbarossa. Would it tell him anything he didn't already know?

Many soldiers who volunteered to fight on the eastern front had written books about their experiences, but this was something different. These Danish historians had examined and written about the events in which he had taken part. But why? To expose, to punish? To condemn everyone who had been involved? My father has the book wrapped and hurries home. Now his bookshelf contains yet another book about his war.

This was the book that was supposed to make me understand him better. He had been expecting that the silence between us would be broken, that I would come one day and ask the difficult questions: "Why, Dad? Why did you do it? How could you end up like that?"

Deep inside him there was perhaps also a wish that I might help him move on in life before it was too late. Not only that—he clearly wished that at some point I would take him to task for the catastrophe he had been a part of. After all, to do so would mean that I still cared about him and fully acknowledged my attachment to him. And perhaps we might find a way back to each other again. In any case, that was how I wanted to understand it.

So much from the war years was pent up inside him, gnawing at him. He wanted to let it all out, to try to understand himself and the course his life had taken. The war was not history for him; it didn't end in 1945. He lived in the shadow of the war and the Holocaust, the same shadow I had grown up in. We had something in common; he had always known that. Even though we had never spoken about the war, he was sure that at some point I would flip through his books after he had passed away. It was a big risk, but he took it.

He devoured *Under the Swastika and the Danish Flag*, in which the historians describe how Danish and Norwegian soldiers took part in the killings and atrocities against the civil population of Ukraine. He himself had been there. He made notes and put exclamation points in the margins, underlined sentences and filled small pieces of paper with comments. On one of those, he addressed me directly: "Bjørn! To you and anyone else who might read this—don't believe everything written in it! Like others who write about the war, the authors haven't always kept to the truth!"

Early in the book, he underlined this sentence: "The strict discipline in the Waffen-SS meant that desertion was often synonymous with a death sentence." He also marked the sentence with an exclamation point, and he continued in that way throughout the book. On page after page, he commented with exclamation points or question marks, writing "hmm" or "what!" when the authors discussed places where Regiment Nordland had been or when he had a sense of recognition. Next to a picture that showed two soldiers from the SS Division Wiking without helmets, he wrote, "Where are the helmets?" On a piece of paper, he commented on the way the prisoners were treated: "I always felt 'small' and helpless in the face of those poor men who were taken captive, who thirsted in the heat and froze to ice in the cold of winter (as did we)." Another note read: "I do not fully recognize myself in many parts of this."

Not "fully"? Then he must have recognized something. At the same time, there were many things on which he did *not* comment. The Norwegian soldiers must also have taken part in the abuses the Danish historians describe, but he made no comments on those pages, except for an event that occurred on July 2, 1941, when soldiers from Division Wiking, according to the book, shot civilians and prisoners of war on the road between Lviv and a town farther east in Western Ukraine. Here he wrote, "What?!"

Four years after my father purchased *Under the Swastika and the Danish Flag* at Berntzen's Bookshop, I got a copy for myself. I didn't realize then that my father had already owned the book for quite a while. He was ahead of me—several editions ahead. At the time, I didn't fully understand how caught up in the war he still was. The first cassette recording I received, in 1996, hinted at something, but not very much. I didn't know how much of the war he actually remembered or if he simply wanted to forget. The war had been something we didn't really talk about, not even when I was growing up. My father's war was a trauma that had eclipsed our entire family.

~

It was not until 2004 that I was truly prepared to tackle my father's past. Two years earlier, I had written a book about World War II and the atrocities committed against the Norwegian Jews, although I had deliberately avoided researching what my own father had done.

When I was clearing out his books, I realized that my father had long believed that I wanted to scrutinize his war experiences. That was in 2005, after he moved out of the Torggata apartment. It struck me then how far-sighted he had been and how important it was to him that I take an interest in his life story. I found *Under the Swastika and the Danish Flag* in a crate of books, along with the enclosed messages to me. The crate of books was a chest full of secrets, like the wooden box from Ukraine. He was sure that I would also open that one day.

I never dared to ask my father how it had come into his possession, that little wooden box with carved rosettes and a rose-patterned lining under the lid. It stood high up on the blue bookcase he had built, which in turn stood on top of a wardrobe in the living room. Beneath it he had hung a picture of Knut Hamsun, the writer he idolized.

My father had claimed that the wooden box was from Russia and that he had brought it home from there himself. Not until much later did I find out that it wasn't from Russia but rather Ukraine. There had always been something special about that wooden box, something magical and frightening. We didn't talk about it—it just sat there, a symbol of the locked-up history of my father's war, which for so many years I wasn't willing or able to open.

My mother wasn't afraid of the wooden box or the story that connected it to us. She used it to hold some of her old photographs. One of them showed my father as a twenty-two- or twenty-three-year-old. His hair is cut short at the ears and combed back in waves. His forehead is high, his face long, and there is a hint of a smile around his lips. You can just barely see the top part of his shirt and what looks like the collar of a uniform jacket. The picture was taken by a photographer in Gjøvik and shows my father wearing a German uniform. My mother had tried to crop it out. She wasn't ashamed that she had met him during the war, but she could never get used to the uniform he chose to wear.

My mother was given the little wooden box after their divorce, when my father didn't want it anymore. After she died, I hid it away in a cabinet until the time was right to take it out.

PART I

CHAPTER 1

The Attack

Evening after evening, Petter would lie with the radio pressed against his ear. He was listening to recordings of Adolf Hitler's speeches, broadcast around the world by Deutsche Rundfunk. It felt as though Hitler was speaking directly to him. The failed artist turned politician had a message that reached this young man in the small industrial town of Raufoss in the district of West Toten in eastern Norway. A young man in search of another life, a meaningful one.

Petter inhaled each word, each rhetorical pause. He couldn't understand everything, but he could feel the mood and the allure created by Hitler's powerful and staccato voice, as he spoke into the microphone to thousands of his followers.

There, outside the town center of Raufoss, on the second floor of a small wooden house known as Engeli, the voice of Germany helped turn a teenager into a National Socialist. Petter later explained: "From 1936 on, I listened to German radio, and with my inadequate school German I followed the evening and nighttime news reports; I learned that the Germans had raised themselves up from the ruins. Through the radio, I could be a part of the Germans' *Sieg Heil! Sieg Heil!*"[1]

Germany promised peace, jobs, harmony, social equality, justice—and no communism. Petter thought that Hitler had the right solution, and there were many others who shared that opinion. One of them was Victor Mogens, who until 1937 was the foreign affairs commentator on NRK, the Norwegian public radio company. Mogens was known for his positive reports on the new Germany. He belonged to the right-wing Fatherland League [Fedrelandslaget] and was staunchly anticommunist.[2]

Then Hitler's men came to Raufoss, with their tanks and weapons.

From somewhere deep inside his slumber, he heard his mother shouting, "Petter! Petter! This is war! Wake up! The Germans have attacked Norway!" He opened his eyes and saw his mother standing there. What did she just say? He woke up to a nightmare; it felt like the world was about to collapse around him. He looked up at her, and she said it again. German troops had come ashore on Norwegian soil; they were already heading north. He buried his head under the duvet. It was 7:30 in the morning on April 9, 1940, and Petter had only slept for an hour. The night shift ended at 6:00 a.m. at Raufoss Ammunition Factory, where he worked, and he had only made it to bed around half past six on this Tuesday morning. But now the night was over, and he was awake again. His mother stood in despair in front of the bed, shocked by the awful news on the radio: Norway was at war. What would happen to Raufoss? The industrial town, located 110 kilometers north of Oslo and 12 kilometers south of Gjøvik, was bordered on all sides by farms both large and small. Raufoss Ammunition Factory, known locally as "the Factory," employed 1,200 workers. The town was especially vulnerable. With its large and strategically important factory, it could be a target for an advancing enemy or a British bomb raid.

Petter writhed in his bed, feeling desperate and abandoned. He cried bitterly, like a tortured animal: "The Germans were supposed to be our friends. This can't be true—how could Germany go to war against us!" A thousand thoughts raced through his head. Germany was the ideal state, but if German soldiers were present on Norwegian soil as attackers, then they must be stopped. The Germans can't just march in and take over, he thought. He would become a soldier and defend Norway. His mother left the room, while Petter stayed in bed, wide awake. He had admired Hitler and what he stood for, but not if he attacked what Petter loved above all else: Norway. He resolved to put up a fight.

~

After a long ascent over the hills, the landscape opens up. A ramshackle barn full of scrap metal, an old wagon, and a sled are all that is left of Vestli, the small farm where a family once tried to build its future. Vestli was right next to Øverbyveien, a road not far from the large old Elton farmhouse.

There, a few kilometers east of Raufoss, the sky stretches high over the wide fields. The land is good for farming if you can manage a large operation. But for a smallholder, things look different: stone after stone must be cleared from the hill, and the frozen ground from the cold winter lasts far into the summer.

Ole Kristian Kristiansen and Julie, née Rustestuen, moved to Vestli in 1918 after they got married and he was hired at the Factory. Julie was from a little forest village called Torpa and was working as a seamstress in Gjøvik when she met Ole Kristian. At Vestli, they had to share the little two-story farmhouse with Ole Kristian's father, Kristian, and his mother, Karen Pauline. The small farm was originally called Eltonstuen and was occupied by tenant farmers until it was purchased from the larger Elton farm in 1909, along with around sixty thousand square meters of forest and thirty thousand square meters of farmland.

Petter lived at Vestli for the first two years after his birth in November 1919. But the small farm would prove too cramped for his family. Petter's oldest sister, Eva, was born in 1918, and his brother, Rolf, was on the way. For that reason, in 1921, Ole Kristian and Julie bought a house for 1800 kroner on Bjerkelandsveien, a road that was closer to the center of Raufoss.[3]

After only four years, Ole Kristian sold the house on Bjerkelandsveien to his twin brother and moved back to Vestli. He needed to help his parents, who couldn't manage the farm on their own anymore. Petter was six years old at that point. His grandfather died a year later. Ole Kristian was now no longer just a farmhand for his father; he was a smallholder.[4]

Ole Kristian worked two jobs; he went to his shift at the Factory, and after taking off his coveralls and riding home on his bicycle on the long road, he became a farmer. Julie had more than enough to do tending to the farm, her mother-in-law Karen Pauline, and especially her children, who seemed to be arriving on a conveyor belt. Another girl, Astrid, was born in 1924, and four years later there was one more child, little Bjørn.

～

The Hunnselva River is the very heart of Raufoss. It brings life to the urban area and the surrounding villages as it runs east toward Lake Mjøsa. The river and the Rødfossen waterfall have served as the foundation for

smithies, sawmills, and industry. The Raufoss Match Factory was established in 1873, and after ten years of operation, it employed seventy people.
Some dwellings and a school were soon built around the match factory.[5]

This development attracted many new arrivals to Raufoss. One of them
was the twenty-two-year-old Knut Hamsun, who in 1880 rented a room
from a factory worker. As Raufoss and Toten grew bigger, so did the demand
for better roads. The future Nobel Prize–winning author was employed as
a gravel inspector on a large road-building project in east Toten. Hamsun
made many friends during his time in Raufoss, one of whom was the mother
of the match factory director. She helped fund his travels to the United
States in 1882.[6] Hamsun's time in the US gave him a new direction in life
and was the starting point for a literary career that would have great significance for many people, including Petter.[7]

Things did not go so well, however, for the match factory in Raufoss; a
series of fires devastated the factory operations and the local economy. But
new opportunities would arise. The tensions between Norway and Sweden
grew in the 1880s and through the turn of the century. Norway wanted
to leave the union with Sweden, but many Norwegian politicians feared
this might lead to a Swedish invasion. The country needed weapons and
ammunition. Any ammunition factory would have to be located far enough
from the border that the Swedes couldn't capture it easily. The region of
Toten offered several possible locations, and Raufoss was a place the Swedes
couldn't reach without considerable effort. In 1895, the Norwegian parliament passed a resolution to take control of the land and properties left
from the match factory. A year later, the Raufoss Cartridge Factory started
producing its first series of 6.5-millimeter rifle cartridges.

In the years before the dissolution of the union with Sweden in 1905,
the factory grew at a remarkable rate. Nearly six hundred workers rotated
through three shifts, laboring to make enough gunpowder and bullets for
the country. As it turned out, there would be no war with Sweden, but a
new era had begun for Raufoss. The weapons industry had come to stay,
and the planning for another increase in production could begin—perhaps
for the next war, which would come in 1914.

World War I provided a boost for Raufoss, as bullets and gunpowder
were in high demand. Norway had declared itself neutral in the great war
that rolled across Europe, but nearly three thousand Norwegian sailors
perished as Germany fired torpedoes at Norwegian merchant vessels that

were carrying goods to their enemies. Norwegian shipowners took risks and made a fortune, as did the ammunition factory.

The Factory provided a living for many people, but it also exacerbated the conflict between the traditional agrarian society and the modern one, with its burgeoning socialism and organized working class. In 1914, there were 240 people working at the Factory; three years into the war, that number had increased to 1,000. Ole Kristian, Petter's father, was one of the people hired as a result of the war.

The end of the war brought hard times for many people in Raufoss, as ammunition is considerably less in demand after an armistice. Five hundred workers lost their jobs. Only after 1922 did conditions improve, when the Factory began to produce items for the civilian market, such as fishing gear, cowbells, nuts, and screws. In 1924, the company's name was changed to Raufoss Ammunition Factory.[8] The Factory did more than provide people with jobs; it had a lot of power in the community, as did its leadership. The factory director was responsible for the schools, the activities of the church, and health care, an arrangement that lasted until 1940. Raufoss was a town controlled by the armed forces and the Ministry of Defense.

As the political situation gradually grew more tense, the communists and social democrats fought bitterly over the right to represent the workers at the Factory. The social-democratic Labor Party [Arbeiderpartiet] emerged victorious from that struggle. Religion also played a big role in the social life of Raufoss; many church organizations worked hard to win the souls of people in Toten. The pietistic Inner Mission movement had an especially strong influence in the area, including among the factory workers.[9] Petter's mother, Julie, was a pious believer, so strict that she wouldn't even accept wishes of joy at Christmas. Every Sunday, Petter and his siblings were required to attend the Salvation Army's Sunday school. Ole Kristian, on the other hand, had more than enough to do in his earthly life; he was a frugal and diligent worker. But then one day his body gave out. He was simply exhausted and suffered from attacks of gout. The illness damaged his heart for the rest of his life. He was never completely healthy again and could no longer manage working both at the factory and on the farm. In the end, the family had to give up the farm.

Ole Kristian and Julie had planned for Petter and his brother, Rolf, to take over Vestli at some point in the future. But it was not to be. Their life's work was gone, and they were left with a bitterness that never faded away.

The eleven-year-old Petter had wanted to be a farmer or a gardener, and it hit him hard when the family lost the farm. At eighteen, he attempted to get it back again, but he had no money. The proud working man Ole Kristian retreated into himself and never really came back. Yet, despite his failing health, he somehow managed to keep his job at the Factory. In 1931, after living in a rental in the center of Raufoss, he purchased the house known as Engeli for 2,600 kroner through a forced auction. He received the money as a loan from the Factory, which provided favorable loans and lines of credit for the workers. But the fact that the Kristiansen family, now going by the name Vestli, had lost its farm and livestock, left an indelible mark.

Petter might have needed a father, a voice to advise him and an ear that would listen. Instead, Ole Kristian was wrapped up in his own thoughts, and the distance between father and son grew. "I never got to hear my father's innermost thoughts," Petter explained. "I only knew him from the outside."

~

Nationalism was intense in the 1930s, as countries competed for a better position in the world and more power. Norway also wished to assert itself—which was supported by the Factory leaders, who were willing to sell ammunition to anyone who would buy it. The important thing was to create more jobs, they argued, and there should be no limitations on what they sold or to whom. In 1934, Raufoss Ammunition Factory exported ammunition to Bolivia, which was then at war with Paraguay. The Factory was then reprimanded by the League of Nations, and in 1935, Great Britain specified that it was no longer permitted to sell ammunition to countries at war or in a civil war, except in the case of a "legal war of self-defense" as approved by the League of Nations. This was hardly welcome news to the Factory leadership.

The 1930s was a time of great transformations and conflicts—between rural and urban, between right and left. In 1933, Vidkun Quisling—who had been the minister of defense in the Agrarian Party governments of prime ministers Peder Kolstad and Leiv Hundseid—founded the National Unification Party [Nasjonal Samling]. Quisling, a person more suited to religious brooding than to politics, hoped to appeal to conservative nationalists. He did not find much success in this, as his fascist-inspired party was regarded as too extreme by most people. But there were those who supported him, including in Raufoss. A group of young radical nationalists started to meet in one of the Factory workers' residences, in a space called the Nicoline attic.[10] One of the Factory managers was interested in politics as well as gunpowder; he allowed the National Unification Party's youth organization to use the Nicoline attic as a meeting place for party members and sympathizers. What was unusual about this, of course, was that the young pro-Quisling activists were meeting at the Factory, which was a state-operated defense company. But in this industrial community divided by class, quite a few people had staunchly right-wing opinions, even at the Factory. Many of the engineers had studied in Germany and remained sympathetic to the country.[11] The nationalistic Fatherland League had several active supporters in west Toten, especially in Gjøvik, only twelve kilometers away. In the local election of 1934, the National Unification Party received 10.9 percent of the vote in Gjøvik and elected four representatives to the municipal council. In the district of Toten as a whole, support for the party amounted to around 3 percent.

Farther north in the county of Oppland, in the village of Torpa, where Petter visited his mother's relatives every summer, support for the party was very strong. The party received 17.3 percent of the votes in the 1934 election, and Torpa was the only municipality in Norway to have a mayor from Quisling's party. In both the parliamentary election of 1936 and the local election of 1937, it received 12.1 percent of votes in the district, after portraying itself as the party for the poor people in the village.[12] The economic situation in the district was dire. In 1928, Torpa was in fact bankrupt, and unemployment was high. The party mobilized against this crisis and argued that "the modern age" was the cause of the problems.[13] In Raufoss, there was a lot of sympathy for the problems in Torpa, and donations were collected for the indebted farmers. The strength of the party in Torpa, and especially the social desolation in the district, played a major role in Petter's political development. What Petter's maternal relatives thought about the party is not known; his mother was certainly also disturbed by the situation in Torpa, but she never brought it up.

Many people in positions of leadership at the Factory knew that the party's youth organization had been meeting on company grounds, in the Nicoline attic, and yet nothing was ever done about it. As a former employee explained, "The group found fertile soil among some of the socially engaged young people in the area."[14] Their excitement about Germany only increased after some members of the Nicoline group went on a cycling trip through the country and eagerly shared their experiences upon their return. Several men from the Nicoline group would later enlist to serve on the German side on the eastern front, but others jumped ship in time and broke away from the party. A good number of these young radical right-wing men lived in an area that locals called Superior Town. It was considered one of the better areas of Raufoss, with a social scene that was foreign to most of the townspeople. The men who lived there were referred to as "nobles." They had a tennis court for the officers and engineers who were part of the company management.[15]

Petter was not part of the Nicoline attic group. He attended some of their meetings but never felt completely at home among the "upper crust," as he saw them. Few of them had a working-class background. Petter shared their opinions to a great extent, but his social background and upbringing were completely different. Although he had grown more radical, neither socialism nor communism held much of an appeal to him. It meant nothing to him that his father always voted for the Labor Party. He had been nursed on the fear of the Soviet Union and anti-Christian Bolshevism.

In 1934, a thirty-nine-year-old bohemian artist and fanatical devotee of the new Germany moved to Raufoss. More than anyone else, Eugen Rygel would push young minds in the direction of right-wing extremism. It might have been Rygel, and to a lesser extent the regulars at the Nicoline attic, who fortified Petter's belief in Hitler. Rygel was a strange figure in many respects. In order to stand out from the crowd, he went around dressed like a Parisian—with a white French alpine hat, a black cane, a beige coat or white jacket, and a bowtie around his neck. He insisted that his name, a pseudonym, be written exclusively in lowercase letters. His actual name was Eugen Rolf Ljungren. The surname came from his Swedish father, but it wasn't fancy enough for the would-be artist with grand ambitions. He came to Raufoss to create a mosaic decoration at the hotel and decided to stay. He started teaching a painting class, found a wife, and, most importantly, an audience. Rygel was a zealous Nazi and a highly gifted speaker. He had been educated in Germany and was excited about the changes that Hitler had introduced after coming to power in 1933.

The charismatic Rygel drew the attention of young people, who wanted to hear him speak about the vast transformations taking place across Europe, where he and his wife, Alvilde, took a study trip each summer. She was a popular language teacher at the middle school, and Petter had been one of her students. Rygel opened up his home, Vildesheim, to anyone who took an interest in his various talents. His dream was to paint a portrait of the führer himself, but his repeated letters to the leader got no response. However, another one of his favorite people, Knut Hamsun, was more willing.

Rygel was an entertaining man and propagandist, but many people declined his invitations, finding him too troublesome and too extreme in many ways. Other people claimed he was a "scoundrel" who manipulated and "bought" young people.[16] But Petter listened to him and absorbed what he said. His friendship with Rygel was important, as the eccentric artist had become like an older brother and a father to him. He was willing to discuss politics with Petter, who couldn't do that at home. Rygel's living room offered a safe place for Petter and his ideas.[17]

Petter did not join the National Unification Party or its youth organization, even though he clearly sympathized with the party. It was almost certainly his mother who kept him from doing so. To her, only a Christian community was acceptable. Why join a political party? She did everything she could to get him involved in Christian work. Why couldn't he join the Salvation Army? No, that was not the right thing for him. Petter was interested in politics, and yet he didn't want to hurt his mother, who meant so much to him. In addition, as a young working-class man, he didn't have much in common with the upper-class types who were members of the youth organization in Raufoss. In a sense, he was on the outside looking in. Petter struggled with doubt and uncertainty in these years as his political views were taking shape. He was a diligent student who did especially well in written Norwegian but was not good at math. And of course, there was so much else to be concerned with at this time beyond just school.

CHAPTER 2

The Transformation

In 1930s Europe, nationalism and fascism stood against communism and socialism, dictatorship against dictatorship. The great struggle that brought Adolf Hitler to power in Germany also came to Norway and to Raufoss, but on a much smaller scale than in the homeland of the führer. The year 1936 was a watershed moment for many people; for Petter it was the major turning point in his life.

On Ascension Day, May 21, 1936, a square in Gjøvik called Nytorvet was the scene of a battle between right-wing and left-wing groups, typical of the sort commonly seen in interwar Europe. The lawyer Johan B. Hjort, a founding member of the National Unification Party, was on a lecture tour and planned to attract a crowd of people to the square in Gjøvik to teach the communists a lesson. Gjøvik, also known as the White (anticommunist) city by Lake Mjøsa, was not chosen at random. The fascist party held a strong position there and could also boast of a highly active youth organization.

Armed with batons and dressed in uniform-like sports clothing, forty to fifty members of the Hird, the National Unification Party paramilitary guard, marched into position. On the same day, the national Workers Federation of Sports [Arbeidernes Idrettsforbund] had scheduled a soccer match between Gjøvik and Raufoss.[1] The match was sped up so that people could make it to the square by 6:00 p.m. if they wanted to. For the same reason, the federation also canceled a track and field event that was supposed to take place in Dokka that day.[2]

Some members of the National Unification Party youth organization and their sympathizers had taken the train from Raufoss to Gjøvik. Petter also wanted to go, but his mother begged him not to. She rightly feared that there would be trouble and that Petter might get injured. In the worst-case scenario, she might even lose him, which she could not bear. Another tragedy had recently struck the family when little Bjørn died, only seven years old.

Bjørn's greatest dream had been to become a famous ski jumper. One day, he was out on his own ski jumping, and he tried to tighten his ski bindings. He used a rusty pair of scissors and was unlucky enough to cut himself. The cut became infected, and blood poisoning spread throughout Bjørn's body. Since penicillin was not yet common, the poisoning couldn't be stopped. In the end, the whole family watched over him at the Gjøvik hospital, where he passed away in late March 1936. The grief at his brother's death hit Petter hard. That was why he didn't defy his mother's wishes and refrained from going to Gjøvik.

In Nytorvet, it didn't take long for chaos to break out. Hjort opened his speech with a provocation: "Countrymen, traitors, monkeys, and other people."[3] The counterdemonstrators started to scream and shout, singing the International and throwing stones. Nearly three hundred of the almost three thousand people gathered on the square were said to have been involved in the fighting. Things got ugly, and one police officer and eight members of the Hird were injured. Trygve Lie, the minister of justice from the Labor Party, very much regretted what had occurred, placing the blame on "the young workers."[4] Seventeen people were indicted after "the Battle of Nytorvet," and thirteen of them received a conditional prison sentence, including four young men from the fascist party. As an extenuating circumstance, the court emphasized that Hjort's speech was highly provocative.[5]

"The Battle of Nytorvet" was a propaganda victory for the National Unification Party. It was part of the fascists' strategy of showing up on the streets to meet their opponents face to face, something Petter saw as a sign of courage and power. The encounter in Gjøvik wasn't the first or the last one. In 1935 and 1936, the National Unification Party arranged other provocative events that led to counterdemonstrations. Young people from Norway's Communist Party and the Labor Party weren't afraid of such confrontations and did their best to put a stop to the National Unification Party's events. On seven different occasions in these years, the state police had to rush in to ensure order. On the day of Pentecost, not long after "the Battle of Nytorvet," the National Unification Party held a large assembly in the town of Tranberg, right outside Gjøvik. Nearly a thousand supporters from eastern Norway came to hear Vidkun Quisling's speech. This time, the event was peaceful, and no counterdemonstrators showed up.[6]

~

The year 1936 was also when the Nazis took full advantage of sports in their propaganda efforts. SS soldiers in black shirts served as security guards for the fourth winter Olympics in the town of Garmisch-Partenkirchen in southern Germany. Adolf Hitler opened the games in February, just as he would do five months later, when the summer Olympics were held in Berlin.

Petter, who followed sports closely, devoured everything he could find about the German Olympics, and he was especially excited about the winter games. To him, the athletic events confirmed Germany's position among the foremost nations of the world. The games were conducted flawlessly, and it was a major victory for Hitler's regime. The twenty-four-year-old Norwegian Sonja Henie also contributed by greeting the German people with a Nazi salute during the figure skating competition. All German participants were required to perform the Nazi salute, but Henie did so voluntarily. She won the competition with a superior performance and became extremely popular in Germany.[7] The sixteen-year-old Laila Schou Nielsen took a different view of the matter. She won a bronze medal in the alpine skiing combined event, but when the two other medalists, both German, gave the Nazi salute, the talented young athlete from Norway refused to do so.[8]

Petter heard about Sonja Henie's victory and understood her actions as a clear sign of support for Germany. His father, Ole Kristian, subscribed to *Oppland Arbeiderblad*, but for that newspaper, the winter games were nothing more than "the Nazi Olympics." Petter thought this was unfair and followed the Olympic coverage in other newspapers instead. The fact that his father's newspaper had such a negative view of Germany only reinforced his support for the country. The workers' athletic organizations in Norway and other European countries boycotted the winter and summer Olympics, arranging their own alternative, which was called the Spartakiad and was held concurrently with the games in Germany. On Friday, February 14, 1936, the lead story in *Oppland Arbeiderblad* was "Johan Bakken from Folldal Wins the 30 km." At the bottom of the same page, in small letters, was the headline "Mathisen Wins Gold Medal"—in the winter Olympics. Bakken had won in the Spartakiad, which took place in Oslo.

Oppland Arbeiderblad remained critical when the summer Olympics were hosted in Berlin. While Norway won the most medals in the winter games, it was now Germany's turn, although not everything went according to plan. The worst part was that the Black American Jesse Owens won four gold medals. Hitler, who gladly saluted the "Aryan" medalists, made it clear that he would not salute any of the "negroes." Enraged, he asked how the Americans could have let any of them win. Owens later claimed, however, that Hitler had waved to him.[9]

On August 7, Norwegian athletes also had a moment of triumph over Nazi Germany at the Post Stadium in Berlin. With all the Nazi leaders watching from the stands, the Norwegian soccer team surprised everyone by eliminating the Germans from the tournament. Germany had simply been outclassed. The loud and joyous Norwegians in the stands made Hitler furious.[10] However, for Norwegians who sympathized with Nazi Germany, such as Petter, the win was taken as proof that Norway was a worthy ally of the new regime.

All things considered, the Olympic games of 1936 were a political victory for Germany. The Nazi dictatorship presented itself as modern and effective. Petter was strengthened in his belief that Hitler's Germany was on the right path. He defended the country against what he saw as biased criticism of the Olympics, and he would later emphasize that the German Olympic triumph was a major factor in his growing sympathy for the Nazi regime.

Politically, Petter was moving farther and farther away from his father, and his support for Nazi Germany was the main reason why. Ole Kristian was a member of the Labor Party with an oddball of a son who approved of the very regime that he perceived as a threat. But since Ole Kristian was a man of few words, there were no big arguments. Petter would eventually figure things out, he thought. There were very few people in Raufoss, if any, with Petter's working-class background who shared his way of thinking. Precisely why Petter chose the path that he did is a complicated question without a clear answer. No one can know for certain what determines an individual's political perspectives and attitudes. It could be a need for social belonging, influence from their friends, the opinions of their parents, fear of outsiders, or fear of change. Or simply a desire to rebel against the status quo. Perhaps opportunism is involved as well—an inclination to do whatever is best for oneself. Many people, and especially young people, yearn for something greater than themselves, something that can provide a sense of belonging and acceptance. Petter was a defiant young man with a strong urge to go his own way. Unlike the rest of his family, he was deeply interested in politics and tried to keep up with everything. He listened to the radio, and he read and discussed issues with anyone who would talk to him. But why did he become so fascinated with Adolf Hitler—not only the person but also his political power? In Germany, the same thing was happening with millions of other young people. Like them, Petter wanted to find a solution to the political crises he observed in his own country and the rest of the world. In Hitler, he saw a man who provided people with jobs and security—and a greater sense of community.

Should he join the National Unification Party? He wasn't sure yet. There were also other options; it wasn't the only party that appealed to young people on the far right. Norway's National Socialist Worker's Party [Norges Nasjonalsocialistiske Arbeiderparti] had been founded in Oslo in 1932 with a radical Nazi agenda; it attempted to present itself as an alternative for "working people." The party quickly established local groups at the most important high schools on the affluent west side of Oslo, despite its proletarian rhetoric, and these groups became prominent high school organizations in the capital. The party also recruited members and activists in other parts of the country. In Petter's home county of Oppland, the party gathered strength primarily in Gjøvik, where it had around a hundred members and sympathizers in the mid-1930s, mostly among high school and college students.[11] One of the leading figures in the party, the journalist Jacob Røken Ødegaard, was from Gjøvik; he took over as its leader in 1939. There were also members in Raufoss, but Petter was not one of them, even though he was exactly the type of person the party hoped to attract with its rhetoric.[12] Once again, the decisive factor seems to have been Petter's concern for his mother. He didn't dare to go against her wishes, at least not yet.

In the years between 1935 and 1940, international tensions increased in Europe as a new arms race began. Italy allied itself with Germany under the leadership of the fascist dictator Benito Mussolini, and in Spain, General Francisco Franco instigated a military revolt to overturn the legally elected Popular Front government. Fascism and authoritarian right-wing views gained strength across Europe. Meanwhile, under the leadership of Joseph Stalin, the Soviet Union had emerged as a great power with vast ambitions. In 1938, the German envoy to Norway sent home a report in which he claimed that "three major lines of power now cross in Norway: the German, the Soviet, and the British."[13] How was Norway supposed to interact with these powers? Petter hoped that Norway would choose the right side. Just imagine what it would have meant if Germany found a willing ally in the north! But things did not turn out quite as Petter had hoped.

Petter was obsessed with the situation in Europe. He supported Franco's side in the struggle that the general called a crusade against the Popular Front government after he triggered the start of the Spanish Civil War in 1936. The government in Spain was supported by communists faithful to Moscow, by anarchists, and by liberals. Franco's side received encouragement from the Spanish Catholic Church and military support from Germany and Italy. The fact that Norway and the rest of democratic Europe took the side of the legally elected Spanish government made no difference to Petter. He thought that Franco was doing the right thing and felt frustrated by the way the civil war was "misunderstood" in Norway. The labor movement in Raufoss and the largest union at the Ammunition Factory stood in solidarity with the Popular Front government. For example, the Iron and Metalworkers' Union at the Factory donated money to the Aid Spain Movement in support of the government and arranged several large meetings under the rallying cry "Against War and Fascism." On July 27, 1936, *Oppland Arbeiderblad* reported that "the [Francoist] rebels are suffering defeat everywhere," and two days later the newspaper wrote, "Everyone agrees that the government is in control of the situation." This turned out to be wishful thinking. Franco ended up winning the war he had started.

Ole Kristian was a union member at the Factory. His son turned against everything that he stood for—including his stance on the important issue of Spain. As a result, contact between the two gradually diminished; they turned their backs on each other. Petter, with his increasingly nationalistic and far-right opinions, rejected the very foundation of the labor movement—solidarity based on social class.

Since 1923, the mayor of Raufoss had come from the Labor Party, although the Communist Party also had some influence in the town. When the Labor Party took a more moderate course in the 1930s, shifting away from communism, the influence of the local communists also declined. This development was fine by Petter, who continued to see communism and the Soviet Union as the greatest threat to Norway and to a peaceful world. The fact that *Oppland Arbeiderblad* wrote positively about the Soviet Union only confirmed how dangerous the situation was. "From Dictatorship to Social Democracy" was the title of an article the newspaper published on July 13, 1936, which discussed the work for a new constitution in the Soviet Union. Among other things, the article stated that "today the future of socialism is secured."

Petter viewed it as deeply unfair that the labor press gave its support to a dictatorship in the east while fighting against the new German state. To him, Germany represented a guarantee of resistance against Bolshevism. Therefore, he couldn't understand it when official opinion in Norway criticized Germany's negative reaction to the Nobel Committee's awarding of the Peace Prize to the radical German pacifist Carl von Ossietzky in 1936. The Nazi regime regarded this as a political provocation, as did many Norwegians. In 1931, Ossietzky had been sentenced for treason and espionage, and he was still imprisoned when the Nobel Committee decided to give him the prestigious award. For Petter, the issue was once again whether you were for or against Germany.[14]

Eager to inform himself about what was happening outside Norway, Petter acquired an English pen pal. She was the politically engaged daughter of a tailor, and the two of them exchanged opinions about current world events. An anti-Nazi, the young Englishwoman tried to influence Petter. She sent him articles and newspapers in English that explained the ominous developments for Jews in Germany in 1937. They wrote to each other for a full year, and they also made plans for him to visit her, but nothing came of it. What might have happened if Petter had been able to afford a trip to England? No one can say, but what she wrote in her letters and the articles she sent did not have an effect on his perspective. Even when the hatred of Jews exploded in Germany, in November 1938, he did not reconsider his support for Hitler's regime.

"A disgrace for humanity. The atrocities in Germany have earned the disgust of the civilized world. Hitler continues to devise new attacks against the Jews." This was some of what was written in *Oppland Arbeiderblad* about what happened in Germany on the night of November 9.[15] The Nazi regime carried out widespread acts of violence against Jews and destroyed Jewish properties, businesses, and synagogues. This incident was given the name Kristallnacht, which refers to the large amount of broken glass from window panes that were smashed. The background for the attacks was that a Jewish teenager had shot and killed a diplomat at the German embassy in Paris. On Kristallnacht itself, ninety-one Jewish people were murdered; by the end of the month around four hundred Jews had been killed and around thirty thousand Jewish men arrested and sent to concentration camps—a quarter of the Jewish men who were still residing in Germany. The German Jews were forced to pay a billion Reichsmarks in compensation for the diplomat's death.[16] Kristallnacht marks the transition from discrimination to direct persecution; the situation for the Jews in Germany was becoming increasingly unbearable.

After Kristallnacht, many people who had shown support for the new Germany ceased to do so. This was not the case with Petter, even though his mother repeatedly told him that the Jews were God's chosen people and thus in need of support. She was terrified by what had occurred in Germany, but Petter wouldn't listen. The German authorities must have had a reason to act as they did, he assumed, and he defended what had taken place. Petter was not alone with respect to "the Jewish question." Antisemitic opinions were common in Norway, even outside of the most pro-German groups.

After Austria was annexed into the greater German Reich in March 1938, conditions for the Jewish people in both countries deteriorated. Should Norway remain a passive observer? The issue was discussed in parliament after the Ministry of Justice pointed out that Norway had accepted very few Jewish refugees. In June 1938, a representative from the Farmer's Party argued in a parliamentary debate that Norway must not become a sanctuary for political refugees and criminals. His perspective was typical of the atmosphere on the conservative side; there were many who would rather not allow Jews into the country. The persecution of Jews and other minorities in Germany and Austria created new frontlines in Norway. One group of artists and intellectuals who wished that Norway would accept more Jewish refugees started a campaign, but this movement had little impact.[17]

In February 1939, around the same time that the parliament was considering the refugee situation in Europe, the question of whether Norway should accept foreign doctors who had emigrated was also being debated.

The issue came up when Karl Evang, the director of health, argued that the authorities should grant work and residency permits to twenty German Jewish doctors. Not everyone agreed. *Aftenposten* took a tough stance and printed letters that the newspaper had received from doctors and medical students who didn't want competition from foreign doctors. "Reckless to Import Doctors," the newspaper claimed in the lead article on February 11. Openly antisemitic opinions were expressed by the protesting doctors and students. On February 23, an anonymous doctor who had been given a column in *Aftenposten* demanded to know whether these doctors were "Marxist Jews." If they were, he considered it necessary to issue a warning: "Has the state not yet understood that it is difficult enough to get rid of a single Jew? And don't the authorities realize that no other country is accepting Jews?" The doctor concluded, "And please do not respond with vague accusations, especially not about fear or hatred of the Jews. That can wait until we have a chance to try them on for ourselves, so to speak!" The only individual Jewish person the doctor mentioned was the former Soviet Bolshevik leader Leo Trotsky, who in 1935 had been granted residency in Norway. Trotsky was a refugee from his own country after getting on the wrong side of Joseph Stalin. The minister of justice, Trygve Lie, expelled him from Norway in 1936 because he was continuing his political battle against Stalin's regime on Norwegian soil.

The debate about the Jewish doctors continued until March 30, when medical students called a meeting at the office of the Medical Society to consider the so-called importation of foreign doctors. The meeting took place only a few weeks after Germany invaded Czechoslovakia and the Jews of Europe were about to be trapped. Even though Karl Evang made it clear at the meeting that ten to twenty doctors wouldn't present much competition for the doctors already in Norway, not everyone was convinced. Of those in attendance, 182 voted against accepting the displaced Jewish doctors, while 115 voted in favor.[18]

∼

The German war machine was now underway. On September 1, 1939, German troops invaded Poland, and two days later, Great Britain and France declared war against Germany. Petter was in favor of Hitler's war, but he wasn't prepared for Norway to be drawn into Germany's war plans. When

German airplanes flew over Raufoss on April 9, 1940, the antiaircraft defense system protecting the Ammunition Factory opened fire. But no planes were damaged and no soldiers were injured, even as the Germans shot back. It was a warning of what was to come. In the following days, the air-raid siren blared repeatedly. It was only a matter of time before the Germans took Raufoss. The initial plan was to destroy the machines and equipment before the Germans arrived, but on April 18, a counterorder came from General Otto Ruge saying that nothing should be blown up. At the same time, the factory leaders received a message telling them to flee from Raufoss with their families. In his memoirs, General Ruge explained that the idea had been to remove "certain parts of the machines, so that it would not take long to restart the factory operations again."[19] That didn't happen either.

The Germans approached the region of Toten and the town of Raufoss from the south. The fateful decision to spare the ammunition factory left it available to the Germans and ready to start production to meet their military goals. On April 20, 1940, German tanks rolled into the center of Raufoss, followed by infantry soldiers. All resistance was to be crushed; civilian hostages were forced to walk in front of the armed forces to prevent any attacks on the Germans.

Petter was at home alone. He went to the kitchen window when he heard loud crashes coming from the road outside the house. The majority of the town's inhabitants had fled, seeking refuge with people they knew on farms in the nearby countryside. Petter's sisters and his mother had gone to Torpa, while he had stayed home with his father and his brother, Rolf. Suddenly, a bit farther up the road, an army tank emerged crossing the bridge over a small stream. Two male figures stood along the road in dark raincoats with rucksacks. Then the fateful moment came: for one reason or another, the two men started to run toward the forest, probably in panic. A pair of German soldiers jumped off the tank and pursued them. Petter didn't see what happened to the two men, but he feared the worst. When the Germans were out of sight, Petter ran out of the house. He found two corpses full of bullet holes. The two men who were shot turned out to be the forty-five-year-old Arne Ninive, a chairman at the Factory, and the fifty-three-year-old merchant Anton Skundberg. "That was my first experience of war," Petter later said. "It was so unnecessary, but they were all so nervous—on both sides."

His shock at what had taken place right outside his home eventually passed. Petter thought that the two men who were killed had acted stupidly. But he couldn't just leave them lying there. He got hold of a sled, and with Rolf's help, he dragged the two deceased men to the cemetery, where the pastor's assistant took care of the corpses.

Petter couldn't wait any longer; he wanted to take a closer look at the German soldiers and maybe even speak to them. He was curious and excited, and he had faith in the Germans—there was no way they could really be the "man-eaters" people said they were. In Raufoss's town center, the Germans had a laugh about the name of Toten Sparebank—"the Savings Bank of the Dead." It was also said that they disliked being served "Toten lefse." Things weren't so funny for everyone: the Germans had already shot four civilians in Raufoss. Petter, however, stepped in as an extra worker at Andresen's Bakery, to ensure the Germans got to purchase fresh baked goods. It was better for them to pay for things rather than just breaking in and stealing, he reasoned.

One day, Petter came home after working at the bakery and saw that the main door of his house had been broken into. A camera was missing, along with all the homemade juice they had stored in the cellar. Petter understood that it must have been the Germans, but despite the fact that they had broken in, he excused them, because "the floor wasn't dirty, no drawers had been broken into, everything was the same as before except a little damage to the door." Even their breaking in to his own home could not change Petter's positive view of the German soldiers.

When the commotion eventually settled down and the Germans were established in Raufoss, everyday life started up again. Petter later explained how his mother had left the white laundry in large tubs of water when she left town. In the warm spring weather, the clothes started to smell bad, since laundry detergent at that time contained animal fats that couldn't be left outside for long when it was warm. Petter took care of the problem. He rinsed the laundry, thinking that his family would return soon and that everything should be in order. Now was the time to adapt to the new situation, Petter thought. Everyone would benefit from that.

When Germany invaded Norway on April 9, Petter had felt ready to put on a uniform to fight against it. He gave up that idea within a few weeks. Now he was "very pro-German" and embraced the idea of cooperating with the occupying forces: "We got used to the Germans, they were very disciplined." He agreed that it was important for the Germans to gain a foothold in Norway, especially along the lengthy western coastline. Germany was at war with Great Britain, and Petter understood Germany's desire to beat Britain to the punch: "If the Germans hadn't invaded, the Brits would have been here."

The "master race" emphasized displays of strength. Throughout the month of June 1940, German soldiers paraded up and down the main street in Raufoss in full military gear. Repeated command calls and the cry "Wir fahren gegen England" were accompanied by ironclad jackboots.[20] Petter was "convinced that the Germans were so strong, so indomitable that they would emerge victorious from any and all battles." For him, the goal was "to cooperate with them as long as it remained possible! The starting point—which was absolutely crucial—was to get so close to the Germans that they had no reason to doubt our intentions or our willingness to collaborate."

Petter had been temporarily laid off from his job at the Ammunition Factory and enrolled in the Employment Service, which had been established by the Administrative Council but had increasingly come under the control of the National Unification Party.[21] He was employed on a farm in Biri, just north of Gjøvik, where he remained until late in the autumn of 1940, when his job at the factory started up again.

Despite his strong sympathies for the National Unification Party, Petter had still not joined it. He postponed doing so again and again. It took a lot to "speak one's mind in a small community." But now the time had come; he had everything to gain by joining the party. On August 30, he received his membership materials as party member number 5350. Other young men did the same thing; like Petter, they had been impressed by the efficiency and organization of the Germans.[22] Petter became an active member of the party and worked eagerly to persuade others to join. Although he had previously stood on the sidelines, he now criticized others for not wanting to participate. No other members of his family were convinced, although he kept trying.

Petter was not the only one in Raufoss who accepted the German occupation. For many people, resistance gradually shifted into adaptation or collaboration. The Germans understood the importance of winning over the workers at the Factory. They introduced more benefits than had previously been available, and the employees accepted them. They offered the workers and their families extra food rations and the chance to purchase some types of food at a lower price. Tobacco plants of "the Havana variety" were also available to order.[23] As a result, people who were lucky enough to work at the Factory had a better experience, in material terms, than most other people in Norway during the war. The number of employees also grew drastically during the war years. The Factory had originally been situated in Toten so that it would not fall into Swedish hands in the event of war, but now it was protected by the occupying Germans, who adapted it to suit their needs. The Factory became a forge for German weapons. The occupiers and their supporters took control of the unions and installed loyal leaders where necessary. This meant extensive cooperation between the trade unions—especially the Iron and Metalworkers' Union—and the company management, who directed the Factory on behalf of the occupying power. Output and sales of ammunition increased considerably in the war years, and the resistance movement was never effective in its attempts to sabotage or halt production.

As early as September 1940, the Administrative Council approved an order from the Wehrmacht for the Factory to deliver a large supply of weapons and ammunition.[24] With this, the Factory received the green light to produce bullets and gunpowder for Germany's war of conquest. The justification for the approval was highly pragmatic: what mattered most was to make sure that jobs would remain. The trade unions in Raufoss agreed. Later, in the autumn of 1944, the high command of the Norwegian armed forces sent an order from Great Britain demanding that production at the factory be stopped. In Oslo, Milorg, the main branch of the resistance movement, went into action and attempted but failed to disrupt the power supply to the Factory; the result was only a short break in operations.[25] The Allies never tried to bomb the Factory; they were afraid that it would hurt the civilian population.

The collaboration between the trade unions and the occupying forces at the Factory resulted in the pro-German manager John Seeberg receiving full support from the Iron and Metalworkers' Union when he applied for the position of administrative director in September 1941. The Germans wanted to remove the existing director, who they thought was not willing enough to collaborate. Aksel Nærli, who was the foreman of the union but not a National Unification Party member, wrote a letter to the party's local leader in Vestre Toten, asking him to help Seeberg get the position.[26] After Seeberg, who was a party member, got the job, it soon became apparent where his loyalties lay. In October 1941, Alf Nielsen, head of the steel works at the Factory, refused to approve an order for cannon parts for the German army. To do so would go against his conscience, as he had relatives in the Norwegian armed forces abroad. This led to a confrontation with Seeberg, and the following day, Nielsen was arrested for insubordination. He was later sentenced and deported to Hamburg, where he remained in prison for the rest of the war.

In January 1942, on the recommendation of director Seeberg, the foreman and secretary of the local division of Iron and Metalworkers Union traveled to Germany to study labor conditions in German industry. The union voiced no objections. Director Seeberg also introduced weekly meetings with employees during which he tried to bring the workers closer to National Socialism. In one of the meetings, he explained what he thought about democracy: "Democracy and Marxism are Jewish in their origin and foreign to the Germanic spirit. The goal of the director is to create a model company, both outwardly and with regard to the reigning spirit of the company."[27]

There were, however, also other opinions at the Factory. Some engineers and other key figures did not wish to continue working there after the Germans took over; they simply left the company. One of them made it to Great Britain, where he penned a strongly critical report about the situation in Raufoss. He claimed that the workers at the Factory worked quickly because they didn't want anyone to think they were sabotaging the operations. The workers didn't see themselves as modern industrial workers, he wrote, but still held attitudes from an earlier age.

They are not very much inclined to activism—the workers thought that they would never let terror come to Raufoss. Most of these workers own their own houses, and some also have a small farm. They feel closely connected to the company, and they have always, one might say, devoted their professional love to the company and the town. Their unity is remarkable, but as mentioned earlier, not of the aggressive sort that one finds, for example, at many industrial sites in Oslo. Overall, to characterize the workers, one might say that they represent, in a good sense, an honest and naïve farming milieu.[28]

It was one thing to adapt to the new situation but quite another to become an active supporter. Petter would stay the course he had started on: "We got used to them. For those of us who were pro-German from the start, this happened quickly. . . . When we saw the Germans walking around at ease, with their hands behind their backs, chatting with the children in Raufoss, they won us over. That's what they did."[29]

But the Germans did not merely walk around with their hands behind their backs. Not even in Raufoss.

CHAPTER 3

The Path to the SS

Three young men stroll up Karl Johan Street in the center of Oslo. From Egertorget Square they can already see the German flag with its swastika flying above the royal palace. What had been the home of King Haakon until less than a year earlier was now occupied by Reichskommissar Josef Terboven. They pass by the palace without saying a word, anxious and excited; only one of them has been in the capital city before.

It is the morning of January 14, 1941, and the three friends from Raufoss have taken the first train to Oslo to volunteer to serve in the war. Norway has been through its first Christmas as an occupied country. Regiment Nordland, a Scandinavian division of the Waffen-SS, has been established to aid in the German war effort, no matter where in the world that might be.

After crossing through the palace park, the friends turn right onto Parkveien, an elegant street on which villas, mansions, and embassies are situated as close to the palace as possible. It is twenty degrees below zero centigrade, and the frost has taken hold—this January and February are the coldest in living memory. The winter of 1941 was called a true Fimbul winter, the great winter that, according to Norse mythology, will come before the destruction of the world. Yet the three friends heading to Parkveien 41B this morning are not afraid of the world ending. They believe that Adolf Hitler's Germany will be its salvation and that Hitler is going to rescue Europe from ruin and racial decline. That is why they allow themselves to be measured and weighed in a mansion that the Germans have taken over. Anyone who wishes to take part in Germany's war must pass the test at this newly established recruitment office on Parkveien. To be weighed and found "too light" would be a crushing loss.

~

Petter believed in the Germans' classification of human beings and deeply desired to fit into the correct category. He wanted Germany to be able to use him in the country's great battle. The office on Parkveien had been given the name Ergänzungsstelle Nord des Ergänzungsamtes der Waffen-SS. The door was open only to "Norwegians of Aryan descent," as they would be joining an army of the foremost people of the "Germanic race." Recruits also had to be "well developed physically and mentally . . . and meet all required conditions."[1] In an article in *Aftenposten* about the opening of the recruitment office, it was reported that "a striking number of academics" were among the volunteers.[2] The three friends from the factory town were not part of that group.

In 1941, the legal age of majority in Norway was twenty-one, but to make things easier for younger men, it was decided that volunteers as young as seventeen could enlist in the army without the consent of their parents. The three friends from Raufoss were some of the youngest in the first contingent of Norwegian volunteers. The average age of those who enlisted in 1941 was almost twenty-five.[3]

The German regime in Norway wanted blond Nordic types for their army—they were to be tall, upright, and Aryan. There was little risk, however, that any so-called non-Aryans would show up at the recruitment office. Antisemitic propaganda had escalated steadily since the Germans had taken control of the state. The Jewish people of Oslo stayed at home, many of them still hoping that the whole ordeal would pass by, and that nothing terrible would happen to them.

A photograph of Petter at this time shows a man with dark blond, wavy hair combed back. He has a sharp-edged nose and a slight smile at the corner of his mouth; he could have been a model in a recruitment poster for the Germanic army. His skull was measured and, along with his friends' skulls, found to be correct both in size and Aryan form. The measurements were neatly written down by the German doctors at the recruitment office. The minimum acceptable height "after turning 17" was 168 centimeters, while a twenty-one-year-old had to be at least 172 centimeters tall. Healthy teeth were required, along with a straight back—physical imperfections were not suitable for anyone who wanted to be part of the human elite. If there was anything out of order, the papers were stamped "Nicht geeignet," and then it was time to leave.

The three friends from Raufoss slipped easily through the needle's eye. They enlisted for one year, with the possibility of extending their service for up to three more years, although they expected the war to be over before long. Volunteers who enlisted for one year received a certificate that entitled them to employment in the Norwegian labor agency. Those who volunteered for two years and "actively took part in this war" were promised ownership of "an existing farm with 60–75 acres of good farming land." Details were not provided about where such a farm would be located; it only said it would be "in the east" and "in a community of people of the same Germanic race."

Even though Petter had been ready for a long time, it all went very fast. He had initially wanted to volunteer for the Winter War as soon as the Soviet Union attacked Finland in December 1939. To justify the attack, Josef Stalin argued that Leningrad required a larger security zone to the west. But Petter had not enlisted at that point—he was afraid his mother wouldn't be able to handle it. His father said nothing, leaving it to his wife: "No, Petter, you are not allowed to go." Since Ole Kristian was not in good health, Petter's mother was overprotective of her oldest son. She had already lost one son and couldn't stand to lose any others. In 1941, however, the situation was completely different; it had been almost a year since the end of the Winter War, and she had to accept that Petter was now an adult. Her pleas and tears didn't work anymore. Petter was fond of his mother, but religion didn't appeal to him, and he felt she had an "unbending belief in the Bible." He couldn't stand to listen to her prayers and praise anymore. She had said many times how bad the Bolsheviks were—they were heathens who persecuted Christians. But still, for him to go war against them was totally unacceptable.

Petter's younger brother, Rolf, was also unsupportive. Rolf had begun to work at the Factory in 1938, when he was sixteen years old, but he wasn't very interested in politics. He couldn't comprehend Petter's plans to volunteer for military service and refused to listen to his arguments. Their two sisters wouldn't listen either, but Petter stood his ground; there was nothing that could stop him. He wished to belong to something greater, something he might find among the soldiers in the army. He had a vision of comradeship and a community united in the fight against an enemy that was threatening Norway.

Before the outbreak of war, Petter had been something of a loner, keeping to himself. Then, just before Christmas 1939, Reidar Seeberg, who was two and a half years older, returned to Raufoss. He had been at sea for several years and had returned home with experiences to share with others.[4] Petter and Reidar had not known each other previously, but now they met and became good friends. Petter looked up to Reidar, who had done what Petter wanted to do: he'd left home and seen the world. They also shared the same interests and the same political convictions. Reidar was a nationalist to his core and could vividly describe the world outside Raufoss and Norway. He thus came to play an important part in Petter's decision. The key issue was to defend Norway against existing threats, and to Reidar, Germany was far from a threat.

Their backgrounds were totally different. Reidar was born in Gjøvik, where his father had been the town's veterinarian, but his parents died in a tragic accident when he was just a small boy. What exactly happened is not known. Reidar was the youngest in the family and grew up with his much older brother John Seeberg, who lived in Raufoss. He did not have an easy childhood or upbringing, so when he was still a teenager he signed on to a ship and set out to sea.

Petter and Reidar were both loners who found camaraderie in each other. Reidar didn't have anyone but his brother, and the only person Petter was close to was his mother. Reidar's brother was like a father to him; he was an engineer and an officer with the rank of captain. When the Germans attacked Norway, both brothers fought on the Norwegian side, but their resistance to the Germans was short lived, and they joined the National Unification Party. In September 1941, John Seeberg took over the position of managing director at the Factory, where Petter's father was a shift worker. However, the class difference between Reidar and Petter meant nothing to them. They were against class struggle—that was communism!

∼

The decisive day for Petter and Reidar came on Sunday, January 12, 1941. That evening they met in the elegant Seeberg family home in the center of Raufoss. The two comrades had heard that there would be an additional radio broadcast and that Vidkun Quisling might speak. The radio was turned on as they drank coffee. They stopped talking when they heard a monotonous voice announce what they had been waiting for: "There will be an opportunity for Norwegian volunteers to join a regiment—Nordland— which will be set up in Germany by Scandinavians. Further details will be announced in the press early tomorrow. In connection with this, Vidkun Quisling will now say a few words."[5]

Their ears perked up. They had often heard his voice. The leader of the National Unification Party had made Norwegian public radio part of his propaganda apparatus; he had even declared a coup d'état over the radio on April 9, 1940. After a short pause, Quisling was on the air, and in a ceremonious voice he told them what they wanted to hear: "My fellow Norwegians, Germany's struggle against England—Europe's eternal menace and warmonger—will soon end in decisive victory. . . . England, which dragged our country into the war, has been forced from the European mainland, and Germany has become the core of a new order of Europe under Germanic leadership." Quisling further claimed that Norway was entering a European "fight for freedom and independence." He urged people to fight on the German side to defend what he called Norwegian honor: "The fate of Europe and Norway will be decided in battle, under steel helmets." Those exact words were burned into Petter's memory. Quisling concluded by noting that "the strength of Vikings is not yet gone from our Norwegian hearts!"

Did they hear that right? Petter and Reidar smiled at each other, perhaps a bit embarrassed. They knew the die was cast. Petter was "instantly wild with excitement." By the end of the evening, they announced by telephone to Oslo that there were two young men from Raufoss who wanted to enlist as volunteers. "We had toyed with the idea at some level, but when the call came, we reacted right away, spontaneously," as Petter later said.

Quisling had been trying to persuade Germany to accept Norwegian volunteer soldiers for a long time.[6] In September 1940, he wrote in a letter to the German Reichsminister Hans Heinrich Lammers that Norwegians should have the opportunity to volunteer for the German army, the Wehrmacht. By the time Germany invaded and occupied Norway, it already had plans to establish an SS unit that Norwegians could join, so this would have happened even without Quisling's initiative. The SS wanted to use foreign volunteers to strengthen its own status within the Germany power hierarchy.[7]

Reidar and Petter had made a decision with major consequences for themselves and their families—and Petter had done so without discussing it with either of his parents. He knew he would not have received their blessing, as Reidar Seeberg did from his brother. Petter's family was not political but simply a former farming and working-class family. No one in his family or his community had ever done anything like this. He was rebelling, striking out for himself. He had become increasingly nationalistic and obsessed with Norway's future in a world of vast upheavals.

Quisling's promise was that the volunteers would be given a place among the "German elite soldiers." It was not just a foreign legion; the men who served would be guaranteed an "honorable future when their service was completed," as *Aftenposten* claimed.[8] Quisling and his party wanted to join the war against Great Britain and "international Jewry." The English and the Jews were one and the same to the National Unification Party, just as the Jews and the Bolsheviks were. The party's interpretation of the political situation was flawed, and there was a further logical inconsistency in their arguments now that Norwegian soldiers could be recruited into the German army. After all, Germany was linked to the Soviet Union via the nonaggression pact of August 1939. Germany had gone to bed with the enemy. The Soviet Union and communism represented the ultimate opponent for the party, so the Norwegians who volunteered to serve Germany were entering into an uncomfortable agreement.

The pact between Germany and the Soviet Union outraged Petter—it had been a terrible blow and an appalling disappointment. How could Hitler agree to anything that would benefit the Bolsheviks? This was a betrayal! Hadn't Hitler called Moscow the center of a Jewish Bolshevik world conspiracy? However, his faith in Hitler's abilities meant that Petter swallowed his disgust. It was a question of holding one's nose—the alliance might be a stroke of tactical genius. It would not and could not last, he hoped.

What Hitler wanted to avoid above all was a war on two fronts, which Germany had experienced when it was squeezed between Russia, Great

Britain, and France during World War I. The pact between the Soviet Union and Germany gave the ambitious superpowers rear cover and greater room to maneuver. It made it possible for the Soviet Union to go to war against Finland in December 1939. As a result, the Soviet border moved over one hundred kilometers to the west. Germany and the Soviet Union had divided up Poland, and the Soviet Union annexed the Baltic states and the western parts of Ukraine, thus securing control over the entire country.

In Norway, it was no easy task to defend Germany's game of intrigue while also being in favor of supplying military support. The Norwegian News Agency interviewed some of Reichskommissar Josef Terboven's ministers of state about the recruitment of Norwegian soldiers.[9] They singled out Great Britain as the major enemy and toned down the enemy image they had previously painted of the Soviet Union. Sverre Riisnæs, the minister of justice, attacked the British harshly and argued that "the Norwegian people must realize that the way forward—both culturally and materially—is possible only if England is defeated. There are many people who have not yet understood this, but there must surely be some enthusiasm about the fact among young people."[10] Gulbrand Lunde, the minister of cultural affairs, claimed that Quisling, by calling for military recruitment, had "raised us up from degradation, and once more given our people a proud place among the nations—may honor be eternally young." But few people outside the ranks of the National Unification Party volunteered for service.[11]

Petter became increasingly convinced that the agreement between Germany and the Soviet Union could not last. Yet there was another problem: he recognized that as a soldier on the German side, he risked fighting against Norwegian soldiers and thus ending up in a situation that resembled civil war. However, he dismissed this problem, reasoning that he would not be the first person in history to face such a dilemma. Most important for him was that he was "an international military volunteer who supported an ideology" he believed in. Another crucial factor was that he genuinely believed Germany would win the war. Anticommunism and fear of the Soviet Union were the key reasons he had volunteered, as was the case for many other recruits.[12] Of course, he understood that Germany had occupied Norway, but in his view, Norway was no longer at war with Germany. An article by National Unification Party member and international law expert Herman Harris Aall in the party newspaper *Fritt Folk* made him even more certain that Norway's war against Germany had ended. What was most essential was to adapt and to accept that Germany was not an enemy but a powerful ally.

~

Three days after the state radio station broadcast Quisling's promise of an honorable future for Norwegian recruits, the three men from Raufoss were on their way to Oslo by train: Petter, Reidar and the much younger Bjørn Eide Sørlien. Petter was twenty-one years old, Reidar twenty-three, while Bjørn was only seventeen. Petter's sister Eva, who was a year older than him, had married Bjørn's uncle, Sverre Sørlien, when she was only seventeen. This meant that Petter and Bjørn were relatives in a sense.

Saying goodbye to his mother was hard for Petter. He was disappointed and surprised that so few men had responded to Quisling's call for volunteers. So he chose to say very little about his plans at home. It would have been much easier if there were more people who had chosen to volunteer. Unlike in the case of his two friends, Petter's entire family was against him, and he was full of dread all night long before he left. When he went to say goodbye to his mother, she hid her head under the duvet. Ten months earlier, it had been Petter who had kept his head hidden when his mother informed him that Germany had attacked Norway.

"Take care, Mom" was all he managed to say before he left. He didn't turn back, even though it was heartbreaking to hear her crying. She was not going to stop him this time. Petter wanted to get away from life in Raufoss, where working at the Factory was the only option. He wanted to go out into the wider world, where, as he saw it, a fight between good and evil was taking place. Even though he was politically motivated, he must also have been driven by a youthful thirst for adventure.[13]

Absorbed in thought but full of nervous anticipation as to what the future might bring, the three young men stared out of the train window. It came as a surprise to Petter and Reidar when Bjørn showed up at the train station. They knew Bjørn's siblings but not him. Bjørn felt strong enough and wanted to fight for what he believed in, just like the other two. The train passed through Eina, Hadeland, Nittedal, and Nydalen before they finally arrived at their destination, Østbanestasjonen in Oslo. Petter collected his small amount of luggage—a suitcase and a rucksack. Now all they had to do was walk up Karl Johan Street, past the royal palace, to the recruitment office. After that point, there would be no looking back.

Petter was still in civilian clothes, but soon he would leave that all behind. He was setting out on a long journey—a journey into history, into the war. He didn't return to Raufoss before leaving Norway but remained in the capital along with his comrades. They were housed in the gymnasium at Rosenhoff school in Oslo until the time was right to deploy them.

~

The podium was decorated with flags and sprigs of spruce, and both German and Norwegian flags hung from the ceiling on that Thursday afternoon of January 30, 1941. Keeping a strict tempo, a German military band played two verses of "Hirdsangen," the initiation song, and everyone who knew the words sang along in the same steady rhythm.

The Hippodrome in Vinderen, in west Oslo, was full of German SS soldiers in uniform and Norwegian Nazis in the Hird uniform. A photograph from the event shows that there were also many participants in civilian clothes. In another photograph, Petter can be seen, just barely, as he is leaning forward to get a better view. Everyone is eagerly awaiting the arrival of Reichsführer Heinrich Himmler, a member of Hitler's inner circle who was responsible for Germany's national security. Himmler had been a driving force behind the Nazi regime's racial policy. Under him, the SS, which had started as a security service for Hitler, was turned into an ideological and military power apparatus, eventually becoming a state within the state. It was this racist and totalitarian organization that would prepare Petter and the other recruits for what lay in store for them.

Many of the newly recruited Norwegian SS soldiers were accompanied by their families. Petter had nobody with him, but what did that matter? For the first time, he was experiencing a Nazi meeting like the ones in Germany, in all its spellbinding power. The Nazi-controlled Norwegian state radio broadcast direct from the meeting. Eyvind Mehle, the network's program director, did not hold back his praise when describing the assembly. "Healthy, strong figures, surely the best human material here in Norway, otherwise they wouldn't be here," Mehle proclaimed with passion.[14] The young recruits were greeted with marches, slogans, speeches, and festivity—they pulled out all the stops.

The Hippodrome was charged with excitement. German discipline and theatrics were set to impress. Not only Himmler but also Quisling and Reichskommissar Josef Terboven, who ruled Norway on behalf of Hitler, made speeches. Himmler and his retinue had arrived in Norway the previous day and visited the monument for the German soldiers who died when the *Blücher* was sunk off Drøbak on April 9, 1940.

Himmler was one of the central ideologues of the Nazi regime, even though he looked more like an accountant than a warmonger, with his narrow face and round glasses. In a hall, normally used for equestrian training, Himmler incited the Norwegians to battle with his quasi religious Nazi ideology. Before he went up to the podium, the assembled crowd sang "Treuelied," the SS loyalty song. The Norwegian public radio station aired the whole meeting on live radio, and the newspapers covered the event and helped spread Himmler's message further: "When a new era is dawning— as with everything new that comes into being in the world—it can only be accomplished through suffering and pain. I understand quite well that there are many people in this country who cannot grasp the higher meaning [of what] has taken place, precisely because of this suffering and pain."[15]

Petter was no expert in German, but he understood the most important points. For him, the meeting was a momentous experience—it was especially exciting to see the great leader Himmler in top form. Himmler concluded the meeting by witnessing the Norwegian volunteers as they were taken "into oath." Himmler, as head of the SS, promised them that they would be allowed to serve in the SS. However, the Norwegians were not informed that German censorship was in full force at this meeting. Quisling's final words in his speech at the Hippodrome were not quoted in the newspaper summaries: "Therefore, I conclude with words said by a German poet to Germans but that could also have been said by a Norwegian to Norwegians and that I say to you: embrace your fatherland. Hold onto it with all your heart. There lies the source of your strength." Reichskommissar Terboven knew he was the one with real power, and he would not allow Quisling to talk about the fatherland. Quisling was utterly incapable of making his mark as Norway's leader in such company. In his speech he made a slip of the tongue and said, "England has led us into war, into misfortune, but this misfortune can perhaps become the greatest good fortune for England." After a slight pause, he corrected this to "for our country."[16]

During the meeting, Petter grew even more convinced that becoming part of Germany's great vision was the right thing to do. He wanted to get started, and in the Hippodrome he and the other recruits were served food from a field kitchen for the first time. It almost tasted like war! The meeting ended with the "Horst Wessel Song" and the German national anthem played at a march tempo. War was in the air, but who were the new Norwegian SS soldiers going to fight against? For Petter the answer was clear: he would fight for Germany no matter who the enemy was. And he accepted full responsibility for his choice: "Many people have portrayed us as having been influenced by our elders, but that wasn't the case. We had no one else to blame—and that is the whole truth of the matter." Petter was convinced that Norway and Germany would establish a powerful alliance together. Indeed, he saw himself as so "Germanic" that he changed his last name from Vestli to Westlie—it suited him better.

The promise of honor and military struggle failed to appeal to many young men. When Petter volunteered in January, he was joined by only 160 other Norwegians. The following month, there were 137.[17] The large-scale recruitment campaign for the Waffen-SS was nothing short of a disaster in light of the expectations. It wasn't easy to convince right-wing Norwegians to support Germany unconditionally when Germany was in an alliance with the Bolshevik regime to the east. In March, the eligibility requirements for volunteers were therefore made less strict. The upper age limit was raised from twenty-five to forty, and being married was no longer an obstacle to becoming a soldier on the German side.

～

On February 5, after listening to an 8 a.m. address by a German brigade leader, the first group of Norwegian Waffen-SS soldiers was driven from Rosenhoff school to Fornebu airport. One division from the Hird and one from the SS came along as an honor guard, and the German military song "Alte Kameraden" was played. The journey would end at a school for recruits outside Graz in Austria, one of several schools where the volunteers from "Germanic" countries received their military training. Petter was chosen as one of around seventy soldiers who were first flown to Aalborg in Denmark. Six trimotor transport aircrafts, Junkers 52s, were made available to fly the recruits.[18] There were also officers with the recruits in the planes. From Aalborg, they would take the train the rest of the way to Graz. Not all the recruits were as lucky as Petter; the rest of them had to travel by train the whole way.

When Petter and his comrades arrived to begin their journey, it was cold, twenty-four degrees below zero centigrade, with the sun lying low over the Fornebu airport. According to *Aftenposten*, there was "warm" enthusiasm among the new recruits that sharply contrasted with the frigid winter morning. At the airport, they had to wait a few hours in the so-called Wehrmacht restaurant due to fog over Denmark. While there, they joined the German "boys" in "a gathering of comrades."[19] According to *Fritt Folk*, they were hoping to "go into battle against England for the Greater Germanic Reich."[20]

It was an assorted mixture of young men in the airport that morning— farm boys, students, and a few unskilled workers. However, the majority of them were city boys who had ambitions to become university students. On their heads, they wore everything from flat caps to ski hats; some wore suits, while others had on windbreakers and sweaters. Petter was wearing his suit jacket, a white shirt, and a coat. Before boarding the airplane, some of them had their picture taken with their arms raised in a Hitler salute.

For the recruits, flying in an airplane was extraordinary; few people had ever done so at the time. They were anxious and on edge about the trip over the Skagerrak to Denmark—after all, there was a war going on. Petter was nervous with anticipation, but he wasn't afraid of flying. He just wanted to continue his journey into the great struggle, toward the great adventure. The airplane rapidly ascended to a height of a thousand meters, took a turn above the district of Asker, and then followed the frozen Oslo fjord to the south.

What Petter and his friends were not told, in all likelihood, was that the Germans were in the process of brutally crushing all resistance in Norway. The day before their departure, three Norwegians in Bergen had been sentenced to death for espionage by a German court-martial. It was a warning sign of what was to come, but Petter had left Norway and Raufoss behind.

And yet it was not quite possible to leave everything behind. What tormented Petter most was the thought of his mother. He knew how worried she was about him, and he had made a promise to himself to write to her, to try to get her to understand that he was doing the right thing. She knew that he had enlisted, but he hadn't told her anything else. He was about to go to war, but he didn't know where that would be or who he would be fighting against. Germany needed him. That was more than enough.

CHAPTER 4

The Soldier Factory

The flight over the Skagerrak strait to Aalborg was uneventful, but there was nonetheless a rumor that spread like wildfire among the recruits who had taken the train to Graz, namely, that the airplane that Petter was on had been shot down by an English jet fighter. Perhaps the people who spread the rumor were envious that they didn't get to travel by air? Nothing happened to the Junkers 52 with Petter onboard. "The workhorse" landed safely in Aalborg, and Petter and his airborne comrades continued onward by train.

Four days later, they were in Wetzeldorf outside Graz.[1] In close-fitting SS uniforms, they inspected the recruits who arrived much later from Oslo by train. It was like they had never worn any other clothes. They had already gotten a taste of everyday life at the SS school: upon their arrival, they were told that obedience, subservience, and order were expected.

Graz, the second largest city in Austria, was one of Hitler's favorite places when he annexed his birth country into the German Reich in 1938. Beautifully situated among large hills and mountains, the city is known for its numerous architectural treasures. With its narrow alleys, its many parks, and the Mur River, which passes right through its center, the city seems like an idyll. This was where Petter and the other Norwegian volunteers were to be trained for battle in the Waffen-SS.

The Waffen-SS was not just an ordinary military organization but a league of warriors. Propaganda, antisemitic indoctrination, and weapons training was used to turn young men into elite soldiers. Trainees were taught to do whatever was demanded of them when they were called on. The standards in the camp were impeccable. The facilities were impressive, with two-story brick buildings, sleeping halls that had room for ten men each, and modern school buildings and training grounds. A well-maintained garden with trees surrounded the facilities. The large exercise field was covered with red gravel and referred to as "Red Square." Upon arrival, the recruits were lined up there, sorted by height, and then ordered to the clothing depot, where uniforms, boots, and other equipment were distributed.

But this was no vacation resort; from the start, Petter and the other re-cruits were forced to complete backbreaking workouts and exercises. Speak-ing Norwegian to each other was forbidden. In a letter to his brother, Rolf, written two weeks after he arrived in Graz, Petter mentioned the demand-ing routine but also expressed excitement about his new life: "I hope you understand my scribbling, since I'm tired as a dog after a hard day outside. We had exercises and gymnastics today, which isn't exactly a walk in the park, but it's still a great life. I just wish that you were here too." Petter also asked Rolf to sell some of his clothes, his skis, and a pocket flask, because he was completely broke. At the camp cafeteria, which offered a wide selec-tion of beverages, money went fast.[2]

Petter didn't try to hide the fact that the training school for recruits in Graz was rigorous and intense, but he also claimed that it was a "wonder-ful time." Whether he truly meant that is hard to say. Others thought the training for recruits was more like a living hell than a wonderful time. Some criticisms of the iron-clad discipline made it through the censor, but only long after the recruitment campaign in Norway had ended. The war reporter Per Pedersen was himself a recruit in Graz and later characterized the training as a form of sadism: "We were drawn into a witch's dance, a nightmare of the most devious training methods. Our eyes were dazzled and our ears were ringing; it was as though our bodies were . . . beaten and battered, and the desire to murder radiated out of us, the poor victims of this sadism."[3]

Pedersen nevertheless believed that this hard training was necessary; it made the recruit "an attentive and accomplished pupil." But according to him, the recruits said "time after time" that they would rather live in the trenches for two years than spend two months in Graz. Petter said that the officers were never satisfied, no matter how much the recruits exerted themselves, but he accepted the situation: "It all happened at such an intense pace; in those weeks and months of training, we had mixed feelings. But that's what it was like to train to become an elite soldier." While Petter and his comrades may not have become elite soldiers after only a few months of training, it was nevertheless Petter's dream to become an elite soldier.

A typical day began when the recruits were woken up at 0600 in the morning by a shrill whistling sound that "cut like a knife right to the bone, followed by a cry in the dark that ordered 'Aufstehen! Kaffee fertigmachen!'" Between 0605 and 0630, recruits were expected to attend to personal hygiene, eat breakfast, clean the room, make their bed, and tidy up their locker. Everything had to happen quickly and with painstaking precision. At 0700, the school day began; at this time the recruits got weapons training and learned to sing military songs at a march tempo. Starting at 0800, training and instruction continued outdoors in the fresh air for four hours. Then there was lunch, which was followed by two hours of exercises on Red Square. At 1600, it was time for ideological lessons and classroom instruction.[4] In the evening, there was more training.

This rigorous program was completely exhausting for the recruits. One Sunday, they went to Graz to see the film *Sieg im Westen* at eight o'clock in the morning. Almost all of them fell asleep as soon as the film started. On the way home, they didn't have the energy to sing fight songs on the bus, for which they were punished with exercises.

The recruits were pushed hard, and they were harassed. Their inability to speak perfect German was used against the Norwegians. This bothered Petter: "There was a lot of screaming and yelling in another language." He asked his brother to send him a German-Norwegian dictionary when he was requesting packages and letters from Norway.[5]

Quite different from what the recruits experienced in reality was the tone of the Norwegian short film *Fight under the Victory Rune* [*Kamp under seiersrunen*], which was made to get Norwegians to enlist in the Waffen-SS. Produced in the spring of 1941, this pompous propaganda film depicts the lives of the Norwegian soldiers in Graz. "A world that has outlived itself is now going under in a storm of thunder and crashes," states the introduction to the film, as images are shown from Germany's invasion of Poland. The narrator of the film then claims that "England and Jewry will fall" and that "up from the gun smoke and the sea of flames . . . a new continent will rise" after the battle against "plutocracy and Bolshevism" is won. Long stretches of the twenty-seven-minute film are devoted to the SS school in

Graz. Norwegian recruits are shown, but none are interviewed. It is almost as if they are acting as extras, while the narrator plays the lead role. Nothing was said in either Petter's letters or in Per Pederson's reporting about the systematic ideological indoctrination that took place in Graz. The film didn't mention it either.

In Norway, much was done to portray the German "soldier factories" in the best possible light during the first phase of the war. The 1943 book *Heading Out: Letters from Germanic Volunteers* [*Oppbrudd: Brever fra germanske frivillige*] is a collection of anonymous letters from soldiers from several countries, including Norway, that describe various aspects of their military service, including their training as soldiers. These letters are pure propaganda:

> You can trust us that we have very fine barracks down here. Everything is topnotch and modern. It is going about as well as one could hope. And what discipline! That's exactly what I need! I'm having a great time. The first recruits who came here about five weeks ago have now become completely "Prussian." You wouldn't believe your eyes, if you saw them—especially when one thinks about the recruits back home and then sees the SS recruits here. It's hard to believe that they're both from the same country. . . . Life here is definitely hard, but I like it very much and I'm doing well. If only we had this sort of thing at home![6]

Another Norwegian volunteer in the Waffen-SS wrote: "I have received my training, and I am utterly determined to fight to the last drop of blood. . . . Together we will liberate our country from the capitalists, the Jews, and the Bolsheviks. I know that it might cost me my life, but our struggle is worthy of that sacrifice."[7]

Reichsführer Himmler visited the Norwegian "Germanics" in the spring of 1941, when Petter was still in Graz. It was his first visit since he incited them to battle in Oslo before they traveled south. A photograph shows Himmler surrounded by apparently happy and eager Norwegian recruits. They are pushing forward to get as close to him as possible. One of them looks like Petter.[8] However, it is hard to tell for sure, as they all had close-cut hair and uniforms. All of them looked the same, just like they were supposed to.

Apart from being exposed to Nazi ideology and racial theories, weapons training and field exercises were the most important aspects of the volunteers' instruction before they were sent to war. What the Germans called "Jewish Bolshevism" was designated as the great threat, even though it was Great Britain that was depicted as the enemy, at least so far, and not the Bolshevik Soviet Union.[9]

Anti-Jewish propaganda was ramped up in 1941. The Norwegian Nazis were no different in this respect from their German role models. While Petter sweated and trained to become an elite soldier in Graz, Quisling gave a speech at a large pan-European conference on the "Jewish Question" in Frankfurt on March 28. He argued that Germany's attack on Norway was the fault of the Jews: "The history of Norway in the last generation has seen a rapid growth in the Judaization of all areas of society, a development that was bound by the necessity of natural law to lead to the national catastrophe that came on April 9, 1940, when an attempt was made to pull Norway into the English-Jewish war against Germany."[10]

Quisling urgently appealed to Germany to solve "the Jewish problem" and to bring "the eternal Jew and his divided soul to rest." He continued: "To once and for all put an end to the presence of this foreign, Oriental creature in Europe, we must seize the opportunity, now that the destiny of the war has placed Europe in the hands of a decisive personality." The Norwegian leader argued that Hitler had "saved the peoples of Europe from becoming the prey of the Jews," and he expressed confidence in Reichsminister Alfred Rosenberg and his staff, noting that they "have such great experience and expertise in the matter at their disposal that the problem of the Jews will be solved." Quisling's plea for Hitler and Rosenberg to find a solution to "the Jewish problem" was hardly necessary. Long before this, the Germans had already begun the process of extermination of the Jews in Germany and in the occupied countries. The Nazi regime also wanted to reduce the number of Jewish people outside of Europe, but first more territory would need to be conquered by military force.

～

The time for the soldiers' departure was approaching. On March 11, after a month of training in Graz, Petter and the other Norwegians were sent onward by train for two more months of drills and military training at a new center, Truppenübungsplatz Heuberg, which was in Baden-Württemberg in Germany, in the Swabian Alps, eight hundred meters above sea level.

Already during the first military lineup, something shocking had happened: the volunteers from the Nordic countries and the Netherlands were divided into an artillery regiment and the three regiments of Nordland, Westland, and Germania. The German officers selected the soldiers they wanted from the ranks. The Norwegians had apparently believed that they were going to form a Norwegian army unit, but nothing came of that. The soldiers were assigned individually under German command. The reason for this was that the Germans did not want to have too many troops of the same nationality in a single regiment, because they thought it might compromise discipline and reduce their power. Petter was assigned to Regiment Nordland, while Reidar Seeberg and Bjørn Eide Sørlien ended up in two separate companies in Regiment Germania. Nonetheless, Petter accepted the situation and was proud to be a part of Division Wiking. Each soldier had his blood type tattooed on his arm; Petter received an O tattoo.

In Heuberg, Petter and his comrades took an oath of allegiance to the führer, Adolf Hitler. The oath was intended to bind them to the führer for the rest of their lives: "I vow to you, Adolf Hitler, chancellor of Germany and leader of the Germanic peoples, loyalty and bravery. To the authorities appointed by you, I promise obedience until death, so help me God."[11] Taking the oath of allegiance was a prerequisite for military service.[12] But not everyone had been aware of this requirement, and a few Norwegians were sent home for refusing to take the oath. Even this oath of allegiance was insufficient for the German officers, who didn't completely trust the loyalty of the foreign volunteers and forced them to work extra hard. The young Germans were much easier to manage because years under Nazi rule had left a mark on them.[13]

~

There was something in the air. It became increasingly clear over the month of May that Petter and his comrades would soon be sent into battle, but they didn't know where. The original plan of the high command of the Wehrmacht had been for Germany to attack the Soviet Union in May, but that operation was delayed. On March 25, 1941, Germany signed an agreement with Yugoslavia that led to large demonstrations in Belgrade, and the pro-German government was overthrown. On April 6, Germany attacked Yugoslavia and sent troops to invade Greece.[14] Within a few weeks, both countries were occupied. These delays in the Balkans meant that the attack on the Soviet Union had to be postponed until June.

Petter and his comrades were impatient and unsure of what was going to happen. Some of them started to think that they might not have been needed at all. Others thought that they would be sent to Yugoslavia, an idea that didn't come out of nowhere. Two of Terboven's collaborationist ministers of state, Jonas Lie and Sverre Riisnæs, had themselves taken part in the war in the Balkans after enlisting in the Waffen-SS, although Riisnæs's contribution was modest. He was part of the SS Kriegsberichter company that had been established for war reporters. Jonas Lie, however, held the rank of officer, and spent time in the line of fire. Their participation in the war had a clear propaganda motive: to aid in the recruitment of Norwegian soldiers.

On May 14, Lie and Riisnæs returned to Oslo, proud after their "baptism by fire." They immediately began to spread the message of how fantastic the Wehrmacht was. Lie claimed that the Germans advanced so quickly that "the enemy hardly had any time to fire." He asserted that "the German army will not allow itself to be beaten anywhere in the world." Lie emphasized that he and Riisnæs were accepted as equals by the Germans:

> What distinguishes them is the strength of the Germanic idea, an honest and idealistic attitude toward all Germanic people, whom they regard as equals. The camaraderie these men extended to us northerners came naturally. They met us with warmth and friendliness from the very start; I haven't seen the likes of it—they accepted us completely as comrades.[15]

Lie also wrote a book about his experiences in the Balkans. It is one long tribute to the Waffen-SS, which he portrays as an entirely new type of institution in history: "The Waffen-SS is nobility, faith, and idealism in purified form. The SS men are more than soldiers, they are bearers of an idea, a belief in blood, power, and the future."[16] Lie compared "the dark ships" that had led Norwegian Vikings on their voyages over the sea to the "dark tanks with the SS emblem, the Germanic victory rune," that were now rolling "over the plains of Europe." For Lie, it was clearly important to portray the Norwegian soldiers' participation on the German side as a historically significant endeavor: Norway must help complete the work that the Vikings had started.

Quisling was greatly pleased that Norwegian soldiers were active on the German side in the war. On May 22, 1941, he paid a visit to the soldiers in Heuberg. In one of the photographs from this meeting with Regiment Nordland, it looks as though Quisling is telling jokes—the picture is filled with laughter, joy, and expectation. There are not many cheerful pictures of Quisling to be found, but in this case, it was important to convey happiness, harmony, and togetherness. Not all was well, however. One of the young Norwegian soldiers had taken his life in Heuberg only a month earlier. He was the first Norwegian whose life was lost in German service.[17] Quisling was nonetheless proud of his disciples. The fact that Norwegians had heeded his call to enlist on the German side confirmed his power and his vision. The Norwegian SS soldiers were the incarnation of Quisling's New Norway, in brotherhood with other Germanic peoples. Norway had once again become a nation of Vikings.

Petter does not appear in the photograph that shows Quisling meeting with Norwegians in Heuberg, but he too was full of anticipation. He had become one of Hitler's elites, which he believed was the ultimate achievement for a soldier. "Our honor is allegiance" ["Unsere Ehre heißt Treue"] was engraved on Petter's belt buckle. Although the Wehrmacht soldiers had "God is with us" ["Gott mit uns"] engraved on their belt buckles, the SS soldiers had no need for God—they had Hitler. Their service caps were decorated with a skull. An SS soldier did not fear death and was trained to kill without pity.

～

The front awaited. At the end of May, the new Division Wiking soldiers headed out in military vehicles and by train to the city of Breslau [Wroclaw] in Silesia, which is today in western Poland. The moment of truth for their training had arrived. Manuals about the Soviet Union were distributed to help them prepare. On June 11, Felix Steiner, the head of Division Wiking, gave a speech about how his soldiers should respond to the "dirty war tricks" that they should expect from the "non-Germanic" peoples. On June 19, the time had come to head out. Their journey took them farther east, toward the city of Lublin, only sixty kilometers from the Ukrainian border. War reporter Per Pedersen described the journey: "Like a flock of excited tourists, we crossed through Poland, rolled over the Vistula River in the blinding sun and, with eager curiosity, got out of our vehicles in Lublin."[18] Petter was thrilled that their journey was taking them east, since that was what he had been hoping for.

After arriving in Lublin, the various army units set up camp in several villages outside the city. Pedersen wrote home that there were "many Jews" living in this region, people who "were lulled to sleep at night by the monotonous melody from the ghetto." They were singing "a song of praise to Yahweh, or was it a lament?" he asked.[19] Some of the Norwegian soldiers visited the Lublin ghetto simply to see what Jewish people looked like. In a letter from Lublin published in *Fritt Folk*, Osvald Olsen wrote, "Even in the finest buildings, where wealthy Jews lived, there was an uncleanliness that made you want to leave as quickly as possible, to get as far away as you could from this loathsome race. The Polish people aren't much to shout about either, but I breathed a sigh of relief as soon as I made it back outside the walls of the ghetto."[20] Not long after this, the Germans built a concentration camp in Lublin. Less than two years after these Norwegians were there, most of the city's Jewish people had been killed.

During the stay in Lublin, their preparations sped up. The many vehicles that were part of the motorized regiments were inspected and weapons were cleaned. Their combat readiness was at the highest level. On the morning of June 21, 1941, Hitler's order finally came. The companies were assembled and, standing at attention, they listened intently to the orders from the führer: "The military advance that is being realized at this very moment is, in its scope and extent, the greatest that the world has ever seen." The troops moved farther to the east toward the small city of Rava-Ruska, just across the Ukrainian border. Petter was temporarily appointed as border guard.

Stalin left Moscow on the same evening and went to his country residence, his dacha. At midnight, he was told that a German communist who had deserted and joined the Soviet side had warned that Germany was going to attack the next morning. However, Stalin didn't take the warning seriously and went to sleep.[21] He trusted the pact with Germany to the end. Stalin had also been warned earlier, but he didn't pay heed to that alert either. As early as June 17, a German member of Hermann Göring's staff who worked on Soviet intelligence had warned of an impending attack. Stalin dismissed the report as disinformation and said with an expletive that the German informant should "head back home to his mother" instead of spreading falsehoods.[22]

Stalin also ignored all the warnings that came from the United States and Great Britain about the possibility of a German attack. On June 21, Germany was still receiving strategically important raw materials from the Soviet Union as part of the agreement between the two countries. Stalin did not want to give Hitler a single argument that could be used against the Soviet Union. If he had halted the transfer of materials, it would have been a violation of the agreement.

Petter tried to get some rest as the night turned into morning. Five months and one week after he had left Raufoss, he was finally going to meet the Bolsheviks, with weapon in hand. He wasn't sure if he would ever see Norway again, but he was willing to make the ultimate sacrifice. In front of him lay the border and the great battle.

CHAPTER 5

The Storm

It seemed like the fields had been adorned with the largest sunflowers to greet the soldiers as the motorized troops plowed their way through the vast, fertile plains and passed the wooded hills. Petter was glowing. When Regiment Nordland entered Western Ukraine at the end of June 1941, he felt invincible and was convinced that the war would soon be over.

In the pocket of his gray-green field uniform was the Bible his mother had begged him to take with him. Petter didn't believe in her God, but he couldn't say no to the Bible. It was a reminder of his family and of Norway at a time when he was so far from home. He had no use for biblical words; what mattered now was his will to fight. Petter was an elite soldier, a "Schütze," or rifleman at the rank of private. Later, he would be given the title "Sturmmann," equivalent to private first class in the US army, and he would lead troops into battle.

～

On June 22, 1941, just after three o'clock in the morning, the first regiments of the huge German army crossed the border to conquer the Soviet Union, the realm of evil itself, according to Hitler. Petter and the rest of Regiment Nordland had to wait a while before they could follow; their turn came on June 29. The number of troops participating in the invasion was so enormous that there would have been a bottleneck if all the divisions started at the same time. The world had never seen such an immense military operation; from the Barents Sea in the north to the Black Sea in the south, soldiers streamed over the border of the Soviet Union.

The German attack received support from many quarters. Finland saw a chance to avenge its loss in the Winter War, when the Soviet Union helped itself to Finnish land. The Finns thus entered the war on the German side on June 25. Many Ukrainians regarded the German invasion as a liberation, at least at first, but it would soon become apparent that freedom was not what the Germans were offering Ukraine. On September 17, 1939, the Soviet Union had annexed parts of Western Ukraine, also known as Eastern Galicia, which was then part of Poland. This annexation was possible due to the nonaggression pact, in which Germany and the Soviet Union divided up spheres of interest.[1]

Petter was active in the southernmost flank of Operation Barbarossa. The main part of the invading army consisted of conscripted German soldiers, but there were also volunteers from eight other countries. These volunteers were all in the motorized infantry division called SS Division Wiking, which, as previously mentioned, was divided into the regiments Nordland, Westland, and Germania. Of the nearly 20,000 soldiers in this division, 294 were Norwegians. More Norwegian soldiers would later volunteer to serve in the campaign. The name Operation Barbarossa was inspired by the Holy Roman Emperor Frederick I, whose nickname derived from his red beard. Around 1190, he led a large crusade to Jerusalem, but he drowned when the crusaders were crossing a river in Asia Minor. Hitler did not seem to care about Barbarossa's unhappy end and borrowed the name for his own campaign anyway.

Petter was one of about three million soldiers on the eighteen-hundred-kilometer-long front. Two days after the start of the invasion, *Aftenposten* wrote, "Our soldiers in Regiment Nordland are making Norway's contribution to the defense of Europe and civilization itself. Only now has it dawned on many people how right it was for these young Norwegian volunteers to enlist."[2]

Petter still did not fully understand Hitler's plan to turn Ukraine into a German colony, which is discussed further in the next chapter. On July 6, 1941, Hitler proclaimed that the Ukrainian peninsula, Crimea, would become "the German Riviera" and that he would construct a motorway to get there. His stated goal was to control Ukraine in the way that Great Britain controlled India.[3] Hitler was convinced that the invasion "would be like playing with a sandcastle."[4] In the spring of 1941, he had mobilized the heavy industries in Belgium, the Netherlands, Czechoslovakia, Italy, Hungary, Romania, and the Balkan states in order to produce weapons for the campaign. Later, the Norwegian weapons industry would also contribute, including Raufoss Ammunition Factory.

Germany's allies—Romania, Hungary, Finland, Bulgaria, and Italy—took part in the invasion, but it was Hitler's own oath-sworn troops who led the way. Their belief in their own superiority after the successful campaigns of 1939 and 1940—along with their racism—was enormously consequential for the people who lived in the areas they were now invading. The German officers had received orders to show no mercy or compassion. Hitler made that completely clear when, on March 30, he gave a two-and-a-half-hour speech to almost 250 high-ranking officers from all branches of the military. The army's chief of staff, Franz Halder, recorded in his diary that Hitler specified that this was to be a war of annihilation: "This battle is going to be quite different from the war in the west. In the east, toughness is the same thing as mildness in relation to the future. . . . Our leaders must demand a sacrifice from themselves in order to overcome their misgivings."[5]

During the advance, Petter moved partly on foot and partly in one of the regiment's trucks. He felt safe, and his rifle, a Mauser K98, was always at the ready. It weighed 3.9 kilos, but it didn't feel heavy, and he knew how to use it. Over many hours, he had been trained to load and shoot the rifle, at fifteen shots a minute. If he were attacked, he would respond in kind, without hesitating. That was the law of war. Petter's company in Regiment Nordland included a total of twelve Norwegians.[6] He was in the first company, which in turn was divided into four units. There were about a dozen men in Petter's unit, but he was the only Norwegian. As a rifleman, he was supposed to stay in front and clear the way for the others.

Petter hardly had any time to think; he just needed to keep up the pace. He was well equipped with weapons but not with clothing—he had gray combat trousers, a brown undershirt, a camouflage jacket, and a helmet with camouflage netting. It was an outfit for a summertime war, and it would turn out to be insufficient. He carried a bread bag and a cylindrical container with a gas mask and a kettle. A spade, a canteen, a bayonet, and hand grenades were also part of his equipment. Petter was an elite soldier from Raufoss who was moving into unknown terrain, feeling proud to be "a tiny piece of the army that was advancing into the Soviet Union and thus help-ing to stop the communist takeover of the world."[7]

The soldiers rapidly advanced through Western Ukraine, covering many kilometers each day. The division was equipped with 850 tanks and armored vehicles with antitank weapons. Supplies and soldiers were transported by two thousand trucks of various sizes and models, many of which came from factories the Germans had taken over during their previous European cam-paigns.[8] The problem was that none of them was suitable for driving in the local terrain, and the invading forces could not always use the drivable roads that did exist. Motorcycles and horses were therefore also used to carry equipment and crews.

When the soldiers approached potential enemy forces or a small town, they hopped off their vehicles and spread out in a fan formation. Like light-ning from the sky, they struck down every sign of resistance: "It was like a war of domination. The trucks drove as far ahead as was defensible, we jumped off and carried out a spread offense with artillery and aircraft support. . . . We took over small towns, higher elevations, and patches of forest. After each skirmish, we were back on the trucks again, on to the next stop."[9]

Norwegian war correspondents who had enlisted as soldiers followed along on the campaign and wrote home about what they saw. Although their reports were censored, they still provide insight into what the front soldiers were thinking and what they did. The war correspondent Egil Hartmann wrote about an attack on a Soviet fortification in his first report, which explains what the soldiers did to a Russian man, a "dirty Bolshevik," whom they took captive. They showed no mercy.

> The ones in this bunker were typical Orientals, somewhere between humans and animals in their way of life, as in their mindset. Life does not mean very much to them. The dirty Bolshevik offered striking proof of this. His ambush from behind and his subsequent lies about how there were only five men in the bunker and how they were forced into battle by three officers were what sentenced him to death.[10]

According to Hartmann, there was "no proud defiance, no greatness in his death."

Petter and Regiment Nordland arrived in Lviv, the main city in Western Ukraine, on July 1, 1941.[11] By that point, other German army units had already captured the city. Thousands of Jewish people had already been killed, although Petter later stated that he didn't remember anything about what he saw or experienced there. In contrast, the former engineer Olaf Wahlmann, who joined Regiment Nordland at the same time as Petter, remembered what he saw and wrote it down: "Suddenly, the large crowds open up. On both sides stood elderly men, women, and children with canes and iron bars. Between them, people were pushed forward with words of abuse and beatings, up toward the citadel, which was on fire. The Jews were going to pay for this."[12] Wahlmann also wrote about Jews being thrown out of windows by the Ukrainians. War reporter Per Pedersen, another member of Regiment Nordland, wrote in an article from 1941 that no one took pity on the Jews, since "a number of us" had seen what they had done to the civilian population in the city.[13]

Regiment Nordland stayed in the area between Lviv and Ternopil for several days. Even though the soldiers had survived their baptism by fire, they were still nervous. But they had to keep moving ahead. The campaign was going according to plan, and it was important to take advantage of the momentum. The Red Army had been forced to retreat after major losses. In three weeks, the invading forces had moved six hundred kilometers into enemy territory. The attack had been sudden and fierce. The nonaggression pact had lasted for less than two years, and Stalin had been caught off guard. This pleased Petter immensely, since the agreement with the Soviet Union had been a major source of frustration. It was communism that he wanted to fight against, and now he was doing it.

Petter and his comrades in arms represented the ideal for the Nazis at home in Norway. Each kilometer they advanced was seen as a victory for Nazism and a defeat for communism and Jewry. Quisling and other leading Norwegian Nazis had grand visions of Norway securing territorial possessions in the east. Quisling believed that "even the waterfalls on the Dnieper River have Norwegian names, and our [Norse] gods come from the Caucasus."[14]

On the day after the start of the invasion, the National Unification Party had gathered its supporters on Bygdøy, the peninsula in west Oslo, to celebrate midsummer. Quisling gave a long speech and argued that Norway would be ruled by Bolsheviks if the Soviet Union were to win the war against Germany. He also threw in some antisemitism and Norse mythology, claiming that "Ragnarök is here" and that the Jews held power both in the Soviet Union and Great Britain. "We see the Fenris wolf over in Russia, the wolf in Jewish clothes, and the Midgard serpent in the form of plutocratic Jews over in London. Are these not the evil spirits that will destroy our community of people, just as our ancestors predicted?"[15]

Victory seemed to follow the German flags. By the beginning of July, the first units in the vast campaign had already crossed over the Dvina and Dneiper rivers. The German army's chief of staff, Franz Halder, wrote in his diary that "it is thus probably no overstatement to say that the Russian campaign has been won in the space of two weeks."[16] The same day, Stalin gave a dramatic speech in which he issued orders for the removal of factories and the evacuation of people from the areas not yet conquered by the Germans. From July to December 1941, the Soviet Union evacuated ten million people to the east, nearly half of whom came from the eastern parts of Ukraine. Over five hundred factories were taken apart and relocated, as new industries were to be built on the other side of the Ural Mountains. Thirty thousand tractors and six million cattle were also hauled eastward.[17] Stalin was planning for a long-lasting war.[18]

Petter was inspired and inflamed by the taste of victory. On his steel helmet and his uniform collar SS was written like lighting; he and many others saw this war as a blitzkrieg. He wasn't afraid but rather hardened and focused on his mission as a soldier. The progress they were making encouraged him. It was like he and the other soldiers were intoxicated.

The hero worship in the nazified Norwegian newspapers continued. A group of Norwegian war correspondents, some of them from the Norwegian News Agency and the NRK, the Norwegian public radio station, sent home their reports. Hartmann, who was a contributor to the news agency and *Fritt Folk*, wrote at the beginning of August that the fighting of the Norwegian volunteers showed "contempt for death" and that the company commanders were surprised that "soldiers with relatively little training can carry out such a perfect battle." The commanders were full of "praise and admiration." As Hartman put it, "no Norwegian has brought shame to his country."[19]

But there was another side of the campaign. Petter was surrounded by death. Soldiers were hit by bullets and grenade splinters, and many fell in battle. As he later said, "We experienced victories and defeats. The victories were in many ways also defeats, since even then, many of our men were killed or injured. Way too many young men became torn-apart cadavers." Petter made it through, but it was almost inconceivable that he could "keep running when grenades were taking so many other lives." He still held firm to the belief that his actions were righteous. This comes through clearly in the letters he wrote home to Rolf in Raufoss, where the ammunition factory was now supplying the German war machine with gunpowder and bullets.

The Soviet Union's resistance seemed to be greatly weakened. It looked as if there would be no obstacles on the road over the Caucasus mountains to Baku in Azerbaijan by the Caspian Sea, where oil would provide Germany with new energy.[20] Hitler fantasized about going even farther south, toward the Middle East, to encircle the Allies in a pincer movement, but first the Red Army needed to be forced back all the way to the Urals.

Petter was transformed over that autumn. Earlier, he had gone from being a "person" to a soldier, but now he had become an unthinking implement of war. As he later wrote, "it is only when a front soldier has overcome his own compassion for the enemy that he can, in most cases without hesitating, perform the tasks that are required of him, everything from a calm, almost carefree guard duty in a sheltered position to the most dangerous storm attack."[21] He had experienced periods of hunger and thirst, and it was nearly impossible to change clothes or keep oneself clean. The soldiers marched, slept, and fought in what they had been given. If they got diarrhea, it was even worse than usual. Access to clean water was not guaranteed, and without water, it was hard to swallow solid food. In general, the soldiers' conditions were brutal, and that didn't help make them more compassionate to the enemy soldiers and civilians. Even the days of waiting could take a psychological toll, and waiting was always a part of war. Either they were waiting for a new offensive to begin or they were waiting to be attacked. Petter learned that "waiting feeds fear." He gradually started to understand that the war was not going to be a short one. After three months in the field, he was no longer so optimistic and certain of victory. After a few months of nearly uninterrupted advances, things weren't going quite as he had expected anymore.

~

Villages, fields, and then more villages. Mile after mile, the landscape looked the same. Wherever they went, the invading forces left behind burned villages and dead soldiers and civilians. The first thing the soldiers did when they arrived in a new town was to search for the leading members of the Communist Party, who were called commissars. If they were found, they were executed immediately. The same was true for Jewish people, since Bolsheviks and Jews were the same thing to the German troops.

The war continued to move east. In September 1941, the Ukrainian-Jewish war reporter Vasily Grossman described the destruction wrought by the Germans in highly dramatic terms: "Thousands of German aircraft droned in the sky continually. The earth moaned under the steel caterpillars of German tracked vehicles. These steel caterpillars crawled through marshes and rivers, tortured the earth and crushed human bodies. German officers who had studied in academies led their fascist battalions and regiments eastwards, through smoke and dust."[22]

Petter and the rest of Regiment Nordland were approaching the city of Dnepropetrovsk [Dnipro], which was not far from Dniprodzerzhynsk [Kamianske]. These were two of the most important industrial cities in the Soviet Union, which together produced 12 percent of the steel consumed in the country. It was essential to further German progress in the war that they take control of these cities.

For a long time, Petter had urged his brother, Rolf, to join him in the great battle but to no avail. Rolf probably didn't read the National Unification Party newspaper *Hirdmannen*, which harshly attacked the "Jøssings," a term used to refer to anti-German, pro-English Norwegians. On August 16, 1941, the editor, Orvar Sæther, who was apparently preoccupied with the well-being of women, described in broad strokes what would happen if the Soviet Union won the war:

If the Germanic peoples had not produced an Adolf Hitler, then today our women and children would have been taken captive by Asiatics, mongrels, and slaves, and in the best-case scenario, we would have been sent to Siberia. In the worst case, our noses would be cut off and our eyes would be stabbed out. This simple and basic fact has been understood by some Norwegians, the ones who have volunteered to serve in Regiment Nordland and are today fighting on the steppes of Russia so that the Bolsheviks won't have the chance to cut out the eyes of those pretty *Jøssing* women in the restaurants and cafés, the ones who say such rude things about the National Unification Party and the others fighting the battle for the new era.[23]

Hirdmannen was not the only newspaper that devoted space to the "abuse" directed at the Norwegians who were fighting in Ukraine and on other parts of the eastern front. There were also other outlets of the Nazi-controlled press that did so. In September 1941, the Gjøvik newspaper *Samhold/ Velgeren*, which was read by many people in Raufoss, reprinted a caustic remark from *Fritt Folk*: "Let the *Jøssings* at home be released over there [in Ukraine]. Find them somewhere to run around in their red stocking caps [a symbol of Norwegian anti-Nazi resistance] at night, as long as they make themselves useful in the daytime."[24]

The letters Petter sent to Rolf reveal how bitter he was that more Norwegians did not understand the importance of supporting the Germans on the eastern front. One of these letters was written in an unknown location on the front in September 1941, under miserable conditions, perhaps in a trench or in a house he had helped take over from a family who had been hunted out or even killed.

> What has the mood been like at home since the war against Russia started? Do people think it will be a German or a Russian victory? All of us here know how important it is; if Russia wins, that will be the end of everything we know of freedom or happiness, both for us Norwegians and for all the nations of Europe. Wherever communism has held sway, it has left a path of destruction, but unfortunately, many people at home in Norway are either too stupid or too deluded to comprehend this fact. But the German soldiers know the true story; they've seen the poor Ukrainian peasants who have been beaten down with the scourge of communism. For those people, the advance of German troops is not an invasion at all, but a liberating crusade. And then there are the young people from all over Europe who have joined this final battle against Bolshevik barbarism. Others from Raufoss have also volunteered, you know that, right? It really is needed.[25]

Petter added thoughts about the future: "Even if we don't make it out alive, we all know how necessary it is that at least our descendants get to have a bright and happy future. Even though I can often be superficial and thoughtless, I always consider the children and grandchildren who will come after us; they also want to live a good and peaceful life." At the end of the letter, he asked Rolf, "Are you planning to join the National Unification Party soon?"

~

Though the Red Army had been in continuous retreat, it was far from defeated—there were millions of people to draw on. Three million Soviet soldiers were taken as prisoners, thousands of aircrafts and tanks were destroyed, and 120 divisions had been dissolved. But the weather gods came to the rescue. The autumn rain would soon turn to snow and the grainfields to ice-cold steppes. In the first six months of the campaign, 40,000 of the 100,000 soldiers that the Waffen-SS alone had started with were injured; 13,000 of them were dead. Petter later reflected on the situation in the autumn of 1941: "The frenzied, victorious crusade that was supposed to last only a few weeks or months had ended in a bloodbath, and we were forced to retreat. We were squeezed between troops from the east and the west." Petter's fellow soldier Ola Rishov, from the same division, later explained to him how it felt when the retreat began and the troops had to "give way to the enemy":

> We could see for miles in three directions. Everything looked black from all the soldiers, armor, horses, and canons. It was all moving relentlessly toward us. Our "line of defense" was made up of "Schützenlöcher" [defensive fighting positions] every 150 meters, with two men in each foxhole—Germans and Norwegian, Danish, and Dutch volunteers. Russian grenades were exploding right around us. On our right side, a Russian women's battalion had broken through the defenses of an Italian division the previous day, and we heard that "our" village, where our field kitchen and other supplies were located, had been [taken]. What we didn't know was that the Third Germania (with Arne Borgir) happened to be there on the way out to the front. They demolished the Russian battalion. When we finally received the much-desired order to retreat, it was too late for many of my comrades, but not for you and me.[26]

Even though Petter still believed in the cause, bitter undertones can be detected in the letters he wrote. It wasn't just politics and propaganda anymore. He wanted to get away from the front, at least mentally, and he pleaded for more news from home and for details about life in Raufoss and the rest of Norway. He was sad that he wasn't receiving many letters, either from male or female friends or from Eugen Rygel, the eccentric artist and ideologue he had befriended in Raufoss.

> Well, now I have a cigarette lit, so I can really enjoy myself for a little while as I write this letter to you. I realize that it isn't my turn to write, but if you don't want to, then I'll have to try to scribble out a few words. I'll excuse you for not writing, because I know what it's like. When you're at home with a mother who takes such good care of you every day, you don't think about how much a letter can mean. Only when you leave home do you start to appreciate hearing some encouraging words now and then. And if you happen to find a Norwegian newspaper, it's a big deal. Then you can forget about everything else and imagine that you're sitting at home, reading and relaxing—and you and I both know how nice it could be at home, most of the time. But enough of that, how are you doing, in the grand scheme of things? Staying healthy, I suppose? I am too, for the most part. Of course, everyone feels a little unwell once in a while. But it must be said that I am quite healthy.[27]

Petter wanted to know as much as he could about how life was going at home, including whether they had enough food and tobacco. "I'm interested in all the little things, so when you write back, don't worry about going into too much detail, since the little things are the nicest to hear about," he wrote. However, what bothered him most was his feeling of guilt about his mother, Julie, who he had kept in the dark about his plans. He sent her letters now and then but said nothing about where he was or what he was doing. Of course, she must have realized that he was on the front; she knew where he stood in political matters and how much he supported Germany. When writing to his brother, Petter did not hide his worries about his mother. And his father's bad health was also weighing on him:

> How is Mom doing these days, Rolf? She's probably waiting for me to come home, right? Does she think that I'm serving in the war, or something like that? I can barely imagine how hard it is for her, since she's such a nervous person, but hopefully we'll be on leave soon, certainly by Christmas, if not

earlier. Is Dad healthy and in good spirits? When you write, tell me about all of it. Don't leave anything out.

Julie's situation was different from that of the many other mothers whose sons were on the eastern front in that the others knew where their sons were and felt proud of them. Motherhood had a special place in Nazi ideology: the mother was the unifying force of the family and thus one of the most important cornerstones of society. Women and mothers were expected to give support to their husbands and sons on the battlefield. More than a few mothers wrote poems of praise for the brave front soldiers for Nazi publications in Norway. For example, the poem "Prayer," written by a woman named Charlotte Slattum, describes not only feelings of pride but also of concern. Petter's mother in Raufoss was not the only one who feared for her son.

Lord of heaven and earth, save our sons!
You who made us mothers, hear our prayers!
You who gave us this land,
You who made boy into man,
Make use of him but bring him back if you can.

Lord, we have been humble deep in our hearts.
We learned the meaning of sacrifice for our country.
When they first heard the appeal,
They were eager to volunteer,
And we watched them through our proud tears.

Lord, may you bless Europe's mothers,
Help our sons in battle, fighting like brothers!
There is a cross on the banner,
Of that great army of salvation.
Lord, may you bring it to victory and peace.[28]

But victory and peace were nowhere near as close as Charlotte Slattum hoped. Germany possessed an enormous military, but Hitler's strategic plans were not working. He had overestimated the power of his army and failed to consider the difficult winter on the steppes. In that way, he made the same mistake Napoleon had when he tried to conquer Russia 129 years earlier. The Red Army's ability to adapt to the situation came as a surprise to the Germans. Meanwhile, the factories that the Soviet leaders had managed to take apart and relocate were working again, ready to resume their production of weapons.

Hitler's goal, to reach the rich oil fields of Baku by the Caspian Sea within a few months, turned out to be unachievable. This quickly became clear to the men who were leading the troops in the field, but few of them dared to confront the führer with the truth. A crusade does not turn around, and the promise and oath to Hitler had to be upheld. Petter was neither able nor willing to break this oath; he had made his decision and would never go back. He was part of a firestorm that was going to blaze through communism and create a new world inhabited by a purer race.

CHAPTER 6

Limitless Brutality

Operation Barbarossa, including the invasion of Ukraine, was not the Germans' main objective. The campaign was a means to a much greater end: the implementation of Generalplan Ost, which has been called the most extensive murder plan in world history. The plan involved the colonization of vast regions in the east, and it was contrived by megalomaniacal Nazis with racist theories. The Nazis would implement the plan by reducing the population in the western parts of the Soviet Union by thirty million people. This genocide would be achieved through systematic starvation, through massacres, and by forcing people farther to the east, behind the Ural Mountains and into Siberia. The Jewish population was to be exterminated. Millions of Germanic people—German, Dutch, and Scandinavian—were supposed to take over the territory. The land would be cultivated using slave labor performed by the people who were allowed to remain. Seven hundred thousand square kilometers, or twice the size of Norway's surface area, would become part of the new colonies intended to provide the Germanic race with "Lebensraum."[1]

Generalplan Ost was based on old ideas that, under Hitler's regime, became part of a brutal, integral design. The foundation came from earlier German colonial policies and imperialistic thinking that dated to the 1880s.[2] One of the most important influences in this regard was Friedrich Ratzel, who in 1897 published the work *Politische Geographie* in which the expression "Lebensraum" was first used. He underscored the importance of population growth to revitalize the German people. Around the same time, a pan-Germanic movement was growing.[3] Spokesmen for this movement supported German colonization in the east as a racial "salvation" of the

Germanic people, who were being "poisoned" by the Jews. The fact that in the 1890s, there were around 1.2 million Germans living in the Russian Empire also contributed to this philosophy, known as "Drang nach Osten." Germans began settling in various parts of Russia in the fourteenth century; in Ukraine, there were 500,000 people of German descent. In 1940, it wasn't outlandish to think that Germany might come to the rescue of these German-speaking "colonies." Shortly after World War I, Ukraine had already been designated as an ideal region for German colonization.[4]

During the Russian Revolution, many people of German descent fled from Russia, and around 55,000 of them settled in Germany. A number of these emigrants were influenced by extremist nationalist and antisemitic ideas, and some participated in building up the Nazi movement in Germany. One of them was Alfred Rosenberg, who became a major proponent of Nazi race ideology and antisemitism. He and others argued that race mixing between Jewish and Slavic peoples had destroyed the Russian people.[5]

～

Petter agreed with the political goal of crushing the Soviet Union, but the plan for total conquest, with all its formidable consequences, was unknown to him when he enlisted to serve in the war. He thus became part of this gigantic murder plan without really knowing how extensive it was intended to be.

Petter was a great admirer of the führer, so it would be quite strange if he hadn't taken note of Hitler's anti-Jewish policies, which had of course been a central element of his political message since long before the start of Operation Barbarossa. As early as 1924, Hitler had claimed in *Mein Kampf* that "the struggle against [the] Jewish Bolshevization of the world requires a clear attitude towards Soviet Russia"[6] Now, the war had provided Hitler with new possibilities. In a speech on January 30, 1939, he picked up the thread and went on the attack against Bolshevism and the Jews: "I want today to be a prophet again: if international finance and Jewry inside and outside Europe should succeed in plunging the nations once more into a world war, the result will be not the Bolshevization of the earth and thereby the victory of the Jews, but the annihilation of the Jewish race in Europe."[7]

Petter had left for war after hearing his mother say that the Jews were God's chosen people. He knew perfectly well that the Jews in Germany were being persecuted, but he nonetheless joined the German side, even though he may have had different opinions. If he did, he could not write about it in his letters; the field post office was censored, as he knew. Because of that, there is nothing in his letters to Rolf about what happened to the Jewish population in the areas where his army division moved in, although he did write that the German officers had behaved like "demons" during his training in Graz and Heuberg. The reality he faced in Ukraine was of a dramatically different nature and far more brutal. What he saw there was, in his own words, "ten times worse" than anything from his training. What did he really mean by that? What was he reacting to? Was it the way the soldiers were treated, or was it the way the soldiers treated the Jews? Or was that something he only found out about much later?

~

The Nazis in Norway understood that Operation Barbarossa was not only about the conquest of land but would also have major consequences for the Soviet population. Although not all members of the National Unification Party were die-hard Jew haters, antisemitism was prominent in the party. It was in the songs of the front soldiers. For example, the battle song "I Am a Norwegian Soldier" contains an unmistakable message:

Then we answered our führer:
We will raise all men to battle
Against Bolshevism
Against the Jewish apocalypse.[8]

In August 1941, as German troops were breaking through to the east, Harald Wibe, a leader of the Oslo Unghird (the National Unification Party equivalent of the Hitler Youth), expressed his opinion on the question of whether Jews were humans or animals:

The many prophets of Satanism, i.e. Judaism, have written books that glorify the Jewish race. In these books, the ones the Jews call "goys," which means human beings, are treated like animals, made into their servants. These books show that they believe we are created by God in a human form so that the Jews will have us serve them like animals, and they also believe that God has allowed them to treat us humans, and indeed even our property, in whatever manner they please. Jews are indoctrinated to believe this from a very young age, and this poison is taught to them in each and every synagogue by Jewish "prophets."[9]

Wibe placed the blame for all the atrocities that took place during Operation Barbarossa on the Jews and the communist commissars, who for him were one and the same.

Do the Bolshevik commissars, who for the most part are Jews, not kill women and children? Do they not burn down the property and food supplies of the Russian people? Do they not shoot their own soldiers coldly from behind, if they see that they are fighting in vain and wish to surrender? Is this not proof enough? . . . The Jews call us animals, but aren't they the real animals? Could a human being even do the things that the Jews do every day in Russia? No, only animals, and especially Jewish animals, could act in this way. Therefore, my comrades in the *Unghird*, let us treat the Jews as the animals they are.

This hate-filled young Nazi thought that Norway should follow Germany's example and "get rid of the Jewish influence" or else the Jews in Norway would create the same "hell" as in the Soviet Union. Wibe supported banning Jewish people from most public places and putting up signs that said, "Jews and other animals not allowed."

Wibe's extremist ideas and arguments weren't simply youthful rhetoric. Similar ideas were at the very foundation of Operation Barbarossa. By dehumanizing the Jews in the east while also defining them all as Bolsheviks, it became easier to justify their annihilation.

～

On April 28, 1941, about two months before the start of Operation Barbarossa, the German leaders decided to embed what were known as *Einsatzgruppen* in the campaign against the Soviet Union. These groups would carry out special "security operations" in the occupied areas. In practice, this meant liquidations, specifically that anyone who had anything to do with "Bolshevism and Jewry" would be killed.[10] Each *Einsatzgruppe* consisted of four mobile units that followed the military forces and systematically tracked down and killed the communists and Jews who had not already been murdered. After these specialized squads were sent in, the persecution of the Jews became "systematic extermination."[11]

It was first and foremost the *Einsatzgruppen* who were responsible for carrying out these actions against the Jews, along with police troops and units from the Waffen-SS.[12] However, ordinary Wehrmacht soldiers also took part. General Erich von Manstein of the Eleventh Wehrmacht Army declared on November 20, 1941 that "soldiers must show understanding for the necessity of the harsh measures against the Jews, who have been the driving force behind Bolshevist terror and must pay the penalty for it. These measures are also necessary to suppress uprisings, which in most cases are instigated by Jews, at the first sign of unrest."[13] Adolf Buchner, who served in an SS division on the eastern front, claimed that "virtually all units were involved. . . . It did not matter whether it was Wehrmacht or SS, [or] both of them."[14]

The term "partisan" was soon used to justify the killing of both Jewish and non-Jewish civilians. In Wehrmacht documents, the killing of civilians was described as the destruction of "hiding places, camps, and bunkers used by partisans." In the years 1941–42, over one hundred partisans were killed for each German soldier who died, in what has been called "the bizarre situation of an anti-partisan war without partisans."[15] Even though Jews and partisans were considered synonymous, German military units also used the term "Jews" in their internal reports in referring to how many people they had killed in their operations.[16]

Would it have been possible for Petter to avoid taking part in the atrocities that we know occurred? He himself stated that he thought it was cruel to chase women with children in their arms out of their houses before setting them on fire, but war is war, he thought, and you had to be harsh in the fight against partisans. Petter later claimed that he never knowingly or "willingly shot or used a bayonet against Jews." However, he also said that "Ukrainians pointed out the Jews for them," saying nothing about what happened after that. According to his own account, he was no worse than the other soldiers, so what is reasonable to believe?

Felix Landau, an officer in an *Einsatzgruppe*, was in Lviv on July 2, 1941, when Petter also would have been there. In his diary, Landau wrote, "Shortly after our arrival the first Jews were shot by us. As usual, a few of the new

officers became megalomaniacs; they really assume the role wholeheartedly."
In the entry for July 3, he wrote that his squad had shot five hundred Jews.[17]

The Germans and their Ukrainian supporters fully exploited an event
that took place in Lviv before the German troops even arrived. The Soviet
secret police had killed political prisoners and pro-German Ukrainians
who were opposed to the incorporation of parts of Ukraine into the Soviet
Union in 1939. The German historian Hannes Heer claims that Joseph
Goebbels "seized the chance to present the brutal killings carried out by
Jewish Bolshevism to the international public."[18] At a propaganda conference on July 7, 1941, Goebbels emphasized that "the Jews are to blame" and
that the press coverage of what had happened in Ukraine must make that
perfectly clear.[19] Germany took advantage of "the brutal killings" for all
they were worth: in acts of revenge that took place between July 7 and July
30, four thousand Jews were murdered in Lviv.[20] Ukrainian nationalists
took an active part in these killings.[21]

During the brutal advance of the German troops in Ukraine, some
towns were turned into slaughterhouses, with Jews as the main victims.
One Norwegian soldier, Josef Hansen, a former boxer from Sarpsborg,
later described his experiences. He was part of the Division Wiking's Fifth
Artillery Regiment, which also assisted Regiment Nordland. At a meeting
of the Hird in Tønsberg that he attended once he had returned to Norway,
he shared what he had seen after the troops marched into Lviv in June
1941: "In one place, we got hold of twelve Jews, who we put to work for us.
I've never seen worse workers. It turned out that all twelve of them were
murderers. They were court-martialed and dealt with quickly."[22]

The German Peter Neumann was an officer in Regiment Nordland,
and when the war was nearing its end, he became a company captain.
Neumann survived and was taken prisoner by Soviet soldiers. When he
returned to Germany, he wrote a book about his experiences during the
invasion of Ukraine. The book, which came out in Norwegian in 1959 as
Death's Henchmen [*Dødens drabanter*], is an unsparing exposé of the SS
soldiers' behavior. According to Neumann, the following occurred on July
28, 1941:

> The division has received new orders. In addition to shooting the commissars,
> we are also supposed to shoot, without hesitation, all the Jewish officials that

we find, whether civilian or military. Liquidations, executions, purges. . . . All of these words, which are synonyms for destruction, seem completely banal and bereft of meaning as soon as you get used to them.[23]

On September 23, 1941, Neumann himself took part in a massacre in a small village after the inhabitants were assembled and lined up.

> The SS men have become completely unrestrained. All of the rage that has been built up in the occupied villages in recent days, during the unrelenting attacks from the partisans, has suddenly broken loose. The men have gone insane. Blood is flowing on all sides. These men have been possessed by bloodlust. . . . They are brutal animals who cannot be controlled.[24]

Newspapers in Norway also reported on the Jews in Ukraine. Even these censored reports provided a glimpse of the brutality, although the journalists who wrote them didn't consider the events to be especially brutal. In October 1943, *Fritt Folk* interviewed the acting German press chief, Helmut Sündermann. He openly explained what was happening: "The attempts to gather together the eastern Jews in separate neighborhoods turned out to be unworkable, since these ghettos became centers of criminal activity. So the Jews have instead been gathered into large internment camps where they must work but where they can otherwise manage their own affairs."[25] *Fritt Folk* followed up with questions about the conditions in these "internment camps." In the interview, Südermann also mentioned all the terrible things he thought the Jews had done to Germany and the rest of the world, including what he described as their having taken advantage of the inflation of the 1920s "for the most horrible exploitation of the German people."

The British intelligence agency intercepted German communications and decoded them. These messages show with utter clarity that it was specifically Jews who were being killed by the various military units and by German police. A British report dated September 11, 1941, and titled "German police" states: "The killing of Jews has again been reported in messages sent on August 27, 1941, which refer to areas around the city Kamianets-Podilskyi. The region to the south reports that 914 people were shot, and the leaders of the special forces, who work with Police Battalion 302, report

having shot 4,200 Jews without any losses on their side." The British agent
who decoded this message noted that it was obvious that "police are shooting
any Jews who get in their way."[26] These messages also make it clear which
groups of people were killed: "Ukrainians," "Russians," "Jews," "Jews who
had pillaged," "Bolshevik Jews," "members of the Red Army."[27]

Western Ukraine, or Eastern Galicia, had had a large Jewish population
for several hundred years. From 1821 to 1870, the Jewish portion of the
population grew by 150 percent, coming to represent almost 12 percent of
the overall population. Jewish cultural life flourished through synagogues,
schools, artists, authors, and artisans. By 1939, there were nearly 620,000
Jews in the region. The German invasion tore up everything at the root, as
Hitler not only wanted to conquer but to eliminate all signs of Jewish life.
In the year 1941 alone, 500,000 Ukrainian Jews were killed; over 700,000
were killed in 1942 and 200,000 in 1943. Of this total, 20 percent perished
in camps, while 80 percent were shot by various groups within the German
army.[28] The Jews in Western Ukraine suffered the harshest losses, while
between 30 and 50 percent of the Jews in the central and eastern parts of
Ukraine managed to escape or were evacuated before the Germans arrived.
During the war, approximately 1.5 million Ukrainian Jews were killed by
the Germans and their collaborators. Many others in Ukraine also experienced great hardship; a total of 4.1 million Ukrainians died because of the
war. Seven hundred towns and twenty-eight thousand villages were either
completely or partly destroyed.[29]

On August 16, 1941, the war correspondent at *Fritt Folk*, Egil Hartmann,
reported to the Norwegian Nazis that an important reason that Germany
wished to take Ukraine was for its grain:

> As you know, one of the major segments of the front is located in Europe's
> most fertile and valuable grain-producing region. Ukraine has rightly been
> called the breadbasket of Europe, and one of its most important areas for grain
> production has already been occupied by the German troops. Germany is
> thus not only waging war but also acquiring the enormous amounts of grain
> that will provide bread to millions of Europeans in the coming years.

A financial analyst in the National Party–controlled *Morgenbladet* underscored that not only was grain to be found in Ukraine but also large amounts

of black coal, manganese, oil, hydropower, and fish in the rivers.[30] The cruelty of the German attitude toward the local population comes through clearly in the thinking of the Wehrmacht's central economic office. On May 2, 1941, the office specified that it was necessary for the German army to obtain food "at the expense of" the local population in the Soviet Union. The consequences of this were cynically noted: "Thereby tens of millions of men will undoubtedly starve to death if we take away all we need from the country."[31] A few weeks later, the Wehrmacht's economic experts authored a new document, which stated that it was not only the army that needed food from the Soviet Union but also the rest of Nazi-controlled Europe. The German economists applied a mathematical cost-benefit analysis to the people they ruled over that defies comprehension. One of them, the economist Helmut Meinhold, reached the conclusion that Poland had 5.83 million people more than what would benefit the Germans and what there was room for.[32]

Ukraine was not only intended to be Germany's breadbasket but also a source of enslaved workers. Ukrainians were transported to arms factories in Germany where they replaced the German workers who were serving in the military. In an interview with the newspaper *Deutsche Ukraine-Zeitung*, Reichskommissar Gauleiter Erich Koch of Ukraine declared, "Let it be known, in connection with the Ukrainian population's labor contribution in Germany, that 500,000 Ukrainians have already been released for activity in the wartime economy. The Ukrainians thus make up the largest contingent of foreign workers."[33]

One year later, the number of enslaved Ukrainian workers in Germany had doubled. In an interview with *Fritt Folk* in September 1943, Reichsminister Alfred Rosenberg announced that Reichskommissariat Ukraine had sent "over one million workers to German industries or German agriculture." In addition, over one million tons of grain from Ukraine had been sent to the German armed forces: "Instead of Soviet soldiers, Europeans are now the ones who are eating the bread baked from Ukrainian grain."[34]

Germany was not the only place where Ukrainians were used for slave labor. At the same time that Norwegian SS soldiers took part in the occupation of Ukraine, thousands of prisoners were sent to Norway, where they built the national roads, among other things, that Norwegians still use today.[35] In total, 100,000 prisoners were sent from the Soviet Union to

Norway during the war, and thirteen thousand of them died there. In the period between the autumn of 1941 and the spring of 1942 alone, more than 2 million Soviet prisoners of war, out of a total of 3.5 million who were forced into slave labor in Europe, either died because of the inhumane conditions they faced or were killed.[36]

~

Hitler visited Ukraine while Petter and his division were continuing to advance farther into the country. On August 6, 1941, in the city Zhytomyr, the führer spoke on a variety of topics related to his plans for Ukraine. He wanted the country to become a "garden of Eden" for the Germans, who in turn would protect it from "Asiatic hordes." By the time Hitler and his retinue visited Zhytomyr, SS soldiers had already killed several thousand Jewish people in the city.

Hitler paid another visit to Ukraine a year later. According to Albert Speer, the minister of armaments and war production, who accompanied him on the trip, Hitler underscored that he wanted to turn Ukraine into a German colony and not simply exploit the country in the short term. The colonization would begin with "a systematic population policy," and what Hitler called the New East would be settled by millions of Germans.[37] As early as March 1, 1941, Hitler had explained what he wanted in a speech: "Land that has been won with blood will then be used to make new blood, new families and children."[38]

Germans and other Germanic peoples were thus expected to populate the conquered regions, to build new cities, and to establish estates and farmsteads. The soldiers who took part in the conquest were to receive land in Ukraine after the war, including the Norwegian SS volunteers. Petter, however, had no desire to become a farmer in Ukraine and hoped to return to Norway when the war was over.

Operation Barbarossa and Generalplan Ost also paved the way for Norwegian plans of colonization. More than a few Norwegians saw great possibilities in Ukraine and other parts of the Soviet Union. Several prominent members of the National Unification Party claimed that Norway had historical claims to land in the east. One of them, Olaf Willy Fermann, was a businessman abroad before the war, including in Germany. He returned to Norway in 1939, and that autumn, he traveled to Ukraine with Heinrich

Himmler after they had a meeting in Oslo. The purpose of their trip was to facilitate the enactment of Himmler's plan to "colonize an area in Ukraine with Norwegian farmers."[39] Around the same time, another businessman, Finn Sofus Støren, was planning to establish an area in northern Russia controlled by Norway that would be called "Bjarmland." Støren, also a member of the National Unification Party, had a "Russian office" established for that purpose within the agency he led, which was called the Directorate for Special Orientation [*Direktoratet for Spesialorientering*]. Among other projects, the office began work on a Russian dictionary for use by the Norwegian settlers.

The same people who thought that Norway should take part in the colonization of German-occupied parts of the Soviet Union were also eager to legitimize Norway's historical land rights. For example, Gulbrand Lunde, the minister of culture in occupied Norway, asked the museum curator Eivind Kválen to provide an account of Norway's historical links to the Soviet Union. The conclusion to Kválen's report includes the following claim: "Thus, one can see that there is a genealogical connection between the Norwegians who lived in Novgorod and Finland, similar to the well-known connection between Norwegians in Novgorod, Kiev, and Norway."[40]

In a report to Quisling from November 1942, Alf Larsen Whist, the National Unification Party business ombudsman, wrote, "If necessary, we could of course send some Norwegian farmers to the Ukrainian steppes as evidence of our willingness to cooperate."[41] In addition, a Norwegian delegation traveled to Ukraine to study the conditions there, which resulted in an elaborate plan for a Norwegian colony. Støren wanted a state enterprise under the name the Norwegian-Ukrainian Land Agency to be established, which in his opinion should receive 500,000 hectares of land. He also suggested sending Norwegian craftsmen and production equipment to Ukraine.[42] The Germans wanted there to be industrial activity, but they demanded that they be sent all the products. The Norwegian negotiators, however, made it a condition that all the agricultural products made by Norwegians in Ukraine would become the property of Norway. The conflict was never resolved, and the plans for Norwegian colonies in the east eventually faded away.

Another Norwegian who took an early interest in Ukraine was the minister of police, Jonas Lie. While Petter was involved in the tough fighting in the Donbas region, Lie was also in Ukraine, but farther south, by the Black Sea. He had traveled two thousand kilometers by car to see as much of the country as possible. Lie later described his experiences on this trip in a speech called "What I Saw in Soviet Russia," which he gave at the Klingenberg cinema in Oslo in January 1942.[43] According to Lie, the Jews were "vermin" who had started to migrate across Europe after World War I: "Like a swarm of grasshoppers, they landed in Germany and exploited the unfortunate postwar circumstances; they engaged in financial speculation, they bought things up, they took advantage of the currency and the inflation, they grew rich at the expense of the German people, they spread out like rings in water and took control of the banks, theaters, cinemas, businesses, factories, and free enterprise." Lie praised the efforts of the Norwegian soldiers in Ukraine: "All the German officers, all of the authorities who knew about such things, agreed that our Norwegian volunteers have made a spectacular contribution and shown great personal courage."

Lie also described his stay in Odessa, where the former headquarters of the State Political Administration had been taken over by German-allied Romanian troops. Lie had several "lively days" in Odessa: "It was a few days after the Romanians had captured the city, and early in the morning, Bolshevik agents had blown up the GPU's main building, killing a Romanian military staff member. . . . A state of emergency was declared, of course." What Lie left out of his speech was that the Romanian SS troops, who had invaded Odessa on October 16, went on to kill thirty-nine thousand Jews after an attack on their headquarters on October 22. An additional thirty-five thousand Jews were forced into two ghettos, and fifteen thousand of them died in the next three months.[44] According to an eyewitness, several gallows were raised at various places in the city, where people were hanged to instill fear in the population.[45] While in Odessa, Lie visited the special operations forces that actively took part in these killings, but it is unclear to what extent Lie himself was directly involved.[46] The same Jonas Lie would later become the leader of the organization Germanic SS Norway, which was established in July 1942.[47] That year, Lie helped to plan and implement the deportation of 771 Jews from Norway.

In his speech, Lie claimed that the soldiers he met while traveling were standing tall and that not "the slightest trace of war fatigue [was] to be found; everyone knew that success in the east was as good as certain." He couldn't have been more mistaken.

~

In the autumn of 1941, Petter's feelings of joy about winning were more frequently dogged by second thoughts. He thought about what was happening to the Jews; he was having thoughts a soldier was not supposed to have or at least not share with others. His conscience started to gnaw at him, pushing him to do something he hadn't done before, as he and a German soldier were hidden underground in a little foxhole in October. Darkness had fallen over them, not far from the mighty Dnieper River. The German advance had been halted; they had entrenched themselves as quickly as possible. Something was happening ahead of them in the dark. But what was it? Petter was afraid it was an attack. "Was that the dull rumble of the army tanks approaching? There was something unknown out there ahead of us, something dangerous and murderous. Armored vehicles that made a growling sound, then a deafening roar—we could never get used to it." The Soviet T-34 tanks were made of thirty tons of rolling steel, and the Germans couldn't shoot through the armor on such monsters. They were easy to maneuver and had a maximum speed of forty-five kilometers an hour. It wasn't only the firepower that Petter feared. The Soviet tank operators had also learned a devilish trick: they drove onto the trenches and spun their extra-wide tank belts until they dug into the ground and mashed the soldiers to death.[48]

The two soldiers were hiding in the foxhole, Petter from Raufoss and Mader from Berlin. They were joined together in pan-Germanic brotherhood, but perhaps not quite the way the Nazi ideologues had imagined it, since a true Aryan was supposed to face the Bolshevik hordes without fear. Time passed, and they kept their heads down. What happened to the roar of the monsters? Petter felt ill at ease; a pain was growing inside him. Suddenly, he asked Mader, "Why have you Germans treated the Jews so badly?" Was it his fear of what lay ahead that made him bring up something he knew you weren't supposed to talk about? It was indeed a taboo topic. Petter was scared that Mader might tell the German officers, but he needed to ask the question anyway. It was weighing on him, nagging at him. He didn't like Jews either, but what he had seen in Ukraine went far beyond anything he could have imagined.

After a moment passed, Mader answered Petter's provocative question: "You need to understand that the Jews had way too much power, and there were too many of them in Germany."[49] It wasn't a satisfying answer to Petter, but it didn't surprise him either. He knew that the struggle against the Jews was part of the larger military endeavor that he had signed up for, but now the violence had become too extreme.

Nonetheless, he didn't follow up on his question; he kept pushing ahead. Despite any second thoughts and questions he might have had, he remained dedicated to the purpose of the war. He was trained to be an elite soldier, and it was easier to continue on that path than to attempt to return home. He couldn't give up now.

CHAPTER 7

The Long, Cold Winter

As the dry autumn weather turned to rain, the roads became unusable. This sudden change in the weather, which is common in Ukraine, had not been taken account of by Hitler and his generals in their plans. Everything was soaked and covered in mud. The war reporter Virgilio Lilli gave an almost poetic description of the situation in the German magazine *Signal*.

> In October . . . it began to rain—it came down from violet-gray clouds that were suspended from the sky like gigantic spiders over the troops and the roads—a heavy, slow-flowing water. . . . Soon came the mud, the infernal Russian mud. . . . The deep furrows in the ground were filled with a beer-colored liquid that couldn't even be called water, a liquid that bleakly reflected the thin Ukrainian trees, the clouds, the mud-spattered coats of the soldiers, the gigantic wheels, rifles, and canons. There in the rainy morass, one saw war itself, filthy war.[1]

It was a hopeless task for the Germans who were supposed to drive vehicles full of soldiers, weapons, and supplies. With dark humor, they referred to the mud that made the roads nearly impassible as "Russian asphalt." The situation didn't improve when the snow came, as the report in *Signal* explained: "The snow was white, of course, but as soon as it was on the ground, the mud soaked it in, consumed it and turned it into mud too." The mud and snow formed a thick mass that stuck to the soldiers' boots in heavy clumps that each weighed a few kilos. Trucks came to a standstill, horse-drawn wagons came to a halt. The campaign was reduced to a crawl.

The winter war would turn out to be hellish. No one was trained or equipped well enough for this kind of war. Petter was facing his greatest test yet and had difficulty believing he would pass it. Still in his summer uniform, he had to withstand the wet autumn weather, which then turned to bitter cold. At first, the weather fluctuated between mild and very cold temperatures, which made it easier to get sick. As he wrote much later, "The winter front, a race to save your life. So little to work with in every way! Every problem, expected or unexpected, was against us! Lack of food, freezing cold, dysentery, our old worn-out uniforms—not to mention the hundreds of lice that never left us alone."[2]

In the fifth century BCE, the Greek historian Herodotus described how the Scythians drove the Cimmerians out of the region that is today Ukraine. Herodotus goes into detail about the excruciating winters the Scythians faced: "All the aforesaid country is exceedingly cold: for eight months of every year there is unbearable frost. . . . Horses have the endurance to bear the Scythian winter; mules and asses cannot bear it at all; and yet in other lands, while asses and mules can endure frost, horses that stand in it are frostbitten."[3]

Hitler's elite soldiers would soon experience the intolerable cold described by Herodotus when it arrived in earnest in November. The mud froze into cement; soldiers froze to death like stray dogs. They tried to stuff newspapers and what little grass could be found inside their clothes to prevent the wind from reaching their skin, but that didn't help much. Petter, who was of course used to cold weather and long winters in Norway, swore that the winters at home were nothing compared to the frost in Ukraine. As he later wrote, "I often think that we really faced three enemies on the eastern front, the Russians and at times the Germans and also King Winter."[4] The reason that he included the Germans as erstwhile enemies was that he thought they did not show enough respect to the Nordic volunteers.

～

On November 20, 1941, Division Wiking entered the city of Rostov, also known as "the gateway to the Caucasus." German troops had made it all the way to the mouth of the Don River, where it meets the Sea of Asov on the northern part of the Black Sea. They cut off all avenues of retreat for the Soviet Ninth Army, which wanted to fall back. However, this also marked the end of the German advance on the southernmost portion of the eastern front. Farther north, where the German troops stood only thirty kilometers from Moscow, the advance also ground to a halt. Regiment Nordland and other German troops suffered great losses as they were forced to flee from Rostov on November 29. Petter was part of the first wave of the retreat, and, according to him, they were chased back eighty kilometers to the west when the Red Army went on the counterattack.

The Norwegian government in exile in London and the resistance movement in Norway paid close attention to the fighting in Eastern Europe. News of the retreat was received with both joy and derision. On December 5, 1941, the *Norsk Bulletin*, which was published by the Norwegian Legation in Bern, Switzerland, described the retreat in this way:

> The German Division "Wiking," which consists of traitors from many countries, including Norway, and which has taken part in the German campaign in the east for some time now, is one of the divisions that our Russian allies have forced into a wild escape. . . . As for the Norwegian volunteers in the east, the only thing they are fighting for is Vidkun the Conqueror and the downfall of their own people.

The German field marshal Gerd von Rundstedt, who was responsible for the military in the south, had received orders from Hitler to maintain control over Rostov. After the retreat, he was dismissed from his position and moved to the western front. He was not the only one to fall from grace: Hitler ousted a total of thirty generals who he considered inadequate to the task. Yet the German army leaders had no other choice. The soldiers were exhausted and had given as much as they could. On December 6, they decided that it was time to quiet down until the winter was over. The remaining soldiers of Regiment Nordland waited along the Mius River until March 1942.[5] The troops were going to gather their strength and rotate forces, as they said. Implicitly, it was admitted that not everything had gone according to plan. German propaganda, however, portrayed the situation differently, claiming that the Soviet troops would lose morale in the winter, right when their lack of supplies would start to become critical.

Over the winter, the Germans planned to assemble reinforcements and obtain more equipment. Winter attire was collected in Germany for the poorly clothed front soldiers. According to the National Unification Party newspaper *Hærpilen*, the German textile industry had been working since October 1940 to produce warm uniforms, wool underwear, sweaters, lamb-skin hats, and quilted camouflage caps. Winter huts with paraffin stoves and small electric ovens were also built to be sent to the eastern front.[6]

Domestic propaganda made no difference to the soldiers in the field. The clothes didn't arrive on time, a fatal error that was simply explained away. While the soldiers were freezing to death, *Hærpilen* stated, "The German troops have always been victorious in the winter, and cold winter weather has always helped the better prepared army. The greatest victory ever won by Prussia took place in the winter, just like the German Reich's current campaign. Why would it not be the same this time?"[7] Nevertheless, Operation Barbarossa froze in place. The lightning of the Blitzkrieg had stopped flashing.

Stalin and the Kremlin saw their opportunity when Hitler's troops went into hibernation in December. The Red Army was properly clothed and familiar with the winter terrain, so even though the Soviet Union had already lost over a million soldiers, it went on the offensive, protected by the cold weather and freezing wind. The Germans called the winter "General Winter," and the Soviet Union saw the general as their ally. Over the course of several days in December, the Russians pushed the German frontlines between 100 and 250 kilometers to the west. On December 18, Hitler gave orders for the Soviet offensive to be answered with a counteroffensive. The führer himself had taken over as commander in chief after he dismissed Walther von Brauchitsch, but that did little to change the situation.

~

Petter was on the verge of freezing to death. It was so cold that he could barely sit or stand. His summer clothes had worn thin, and he should have been wearing polar gear. The tall boot on his left foot was practically glued on, and he couldn't manage to take it off no matter how hard he tried. It had been stuck there since the start of the winter. No amount of help from others could get it off, and the skin on his foot was decaying. Both legs were in terrible condition, but the left one was worse. Waves of pain flowed up from his calf, but he still didn't realize that his skin was about to rot while he and his company were frozen solid in a frigid bunker along the Mius

River. There was only a tent cover for the outer door, which did nothing to keep the cold out. It was nearly impossible to get any firewood for the stove.

The soldiers staggered around, desperate from their lack of sleep, while lice bit them and made it even more difficult to rest when they had the chance. Some soldiers had taken a room in a village house, but those were few and far between. With temperatures reaching down to forty degrees below zero centigrade, even before the winter had truly begun, it was impossible to keep up morale. The Soviet army had shown that it could mount an effective resistance, and they attacked even in the harsh cold. While the winter was obviously difficult for the Soviet troops as well, at least they had the right clothing.

Christmas Eve of 1941 was a bright spot in dark times for Petter. The food was a little bit better and there were some songs and candles, but it could not help with everything. His legs were in pain, and he could barely feel his left foot anymore. What could he do? He was homesick, but he didn't want to show any sign of weakness. He was a soldier at war, after all.

Early in the new year of 1942, an officer finally addressed the situation: the stubborn Norwegian required medical attention. On January 10, Petter was sent by horse-drawn sled to the nearest field hospital, which was only a few kilometers from the front. A day later, he wrote a letter to Rolf: "Now I'm lying in a field hospital with my feet frozen solid. It has been quite cold here lately. There is always a horribly cold wind blowing, but now I'm in a calm and peaceful place." As he often did in letters to Rolf, he added, "Do not show this letter to Mom." He wrote a separate letter to his mother, but that one didn't mention anything about his condition.

Petter was not the only one to suffer from frostbite; the eastern front was freezing from north to south. While the most pressing injuries for the Norwegian front soldiers were, unsurprisingly, gunshot injuries received in action, according to a survey of 181 Norwegian front soldiers, about a third of them experienced frostbite during their time of service.[8]

The situation was dramatic. Petter had been taken to a field hospital known as "the slaughterhouse"—and not without reason. Amputations were performed there assembly-line style. Frostbitten legs with the slightest suggestion of gangrene were not worth sparing, and the risk of it spreading had to be stopped. Petter's left leg was in the danger zone, but he wanted to avoid amputation and argued as stubbornly as he could. Two doctors examined his leg right after Petter arrived at the hospital. The older doctor called for immediate amputation the following morning, and he would not listen to any of Petter's protests. The younger doctor, however, seemed to have believed there was still hope. Had he seen the spark in Petter's eyes? He managed to persuade his colleague that it was reasonable to wait and see.

In the end, the inflexible Norwegian in the blood-spattered bed, which had already been used by many injured soldiers before him, got his way. It did mean, however, that Petter now needed to take care of himself. Once again, luck was on his side. The next morning, he was sent to a better hospital farther away from the front, a place that could offer more expertise and care. The train ride there turned out to be a six-day journey in the company of the sick and the dying. It was hell on earth.

> I was sent away on a train packed full of injured and dying soldiers. We were told that the train ride—I think it was going to Dnepropetrovsk—would take two days, but it took six. We were bombed by planes, which made it take longer. I was in horrible pain and the trip was pure misery. We didn't get to eat or sleep at all. When we finally arrived, there was a long stairway up to the room for the sick and injured. They carried me up and took good care of me there. Arriving there was like a dream; there were friendly nurses who talked to me.[9]

Petter had been saved. The immediate fear of freezing to death or of being attacked without the ability to defend himself was now over, although he and the other patients still feared that the hospital would be bombed. Now that the Soviet Union has gained the upper hand, the situation had become dire for the Germans. Even *Hærpilen* admitted in January 1942 that "the fact of the matter is that the dual fight against both the enemy and the Russian winter is very serious. . . . Europe's freedom fighters are making a superhuman effort in the harsh winter cold."[10]

Before Petter had arrived at the hospital, the Germany army leaders had already sent orders for a tactical retreat by the troops north of Ukraine. The Soviet plan, which the Germans figured out, was to encircle and capture a large group of their troops. Fortunately for the Germans, it turned out that the Red Army lacked the strength to carry out this maneuver. Hitler and his men took this as evidence that victory was still possible. But they disregarded the fact that the Red Army had also learned a lesson.

Petter's good luck continued. After a few weeks, a visiting doctor happened to ask one of the nurses, "You have been giving him a saline solution, right?" No, actually, no one had thought to do that. The doctor was outraged, saying that the foot should have been placed in a saline solution from the very start. The nurse was sharply reprimanded, but the foot had improved anyway, so there was no longer any talk about amputating the leg. While in the hospital, Petter was continually reminded of the fate he had been lucky enough to avoid. Next to his bed, a Yugoslavian Waffen-SS volunteer lay with one leg amputated, complaining constantly about the phantom pains he still felt.

A few days after arriving at the field hospital, Petter wrote another letter to Rolf: "They're taking good care of me, and my feet are feeling better every day. I've kept back my tears. The doctor says I've been remarkably lucky."[11] Rolf was also told that he might as well let their mother know that Petter was a patient at a field hospital, since she already knew that he was on the eastern front. Petter was still worried about how she would take the news, and he asked his brother to "make up something to keep her in a good mood."

Petter's fighting spirit was gone, even though his leg had been saved at the last minute. He was thinking it over: should he stay on the front in Ukraine or head home? Given his current situation, he could be released from service, as his leg might never fully recover. He had heard that the SS was forming a new branch in Norway, which sounded exciting. If he wanted to, he could move directly from active military service into this new unit in the Germanic SS. It was going to be a political and paramilitary organization whose task it was to defend the Nazi regime in occupied Norway. Petter though he might even make it home by Easter, but frostbite injuries take a long time to heal.

While Petter weighed his options, his comrades in Regiment Nordland were eagerly awaiting the spring along the Mius River. Petter also longed for the winter to loosen its grip, and he was more than ready to leave the hospital. The conditions there were much worse than he was able to describe in his letters, which were subject to censorship. In one of the surviving letters, the censor has apparently crossed something out. Petter kept the censor in mind and omitted many details. His letters home to Norway paint an idealized picture.

One day, a fifteen-person orchestra visited Petter and the other patients and played tangoes and foxtrots. Even though there were army nurses willing to dance with him, he was still not healthy enough. The musicians could only do so much to stimulate the injured soldiers. But Petter was starting to feel more optimistic. On February 10, 1942, he wrote another letter to Rolf, reporting that the doctors thought his feet looked "decent," even though there was still a long way to go. He was bored from sitting in bed all the time. A week later, the doctors told him that he would be able to stand up soon. He wrote home that he would love to experience the Norwegian spring and that his only source of joy was that a Dane had been placed in the same hospital room. There was probably also a Norwegian soldier somewhere in the hospital, he thought, but it was a very large building, and Petter had no way of finding out where he might be.

Petter's impatience grew. By the end of February, his feet had improved enough that he could stand up and walk around with a cane. The hospital patients had access to plenty of newspapers and reports about the war, but it was all propaganda. There was a clear bias to all the news, and the reporters were just as likely to be soldiers as journalists.

~

The National Unification Party and its youth organization made frequent use of the front soldiers in their propaganda and did everything they could to build support for them among Norwegians. Young soldiers who fell in battle were glorified and idolized. There were plans to construct a memorial hall for the fallen soldiers at Studenterlunden Park in Oslo, next to the national theater. The dead front soldiers were treated as martyrs who must never be forgotten. In the town of Askim, streets were named after two of them.[12]

The obituaries for the fallen soldiers were reverential. In an article in *Austvegr*, the death of a twenty-year-old named Erik was described by a fellow soldier: "His death runestone has been raised among the others. He has marched into the silence—the immortal company."[13] Erik died on the day after Christmas in 1942 while taking part in his fourth campaign.

The article also describes how he was given help to compose a final letter home right before dying.

Norwegian children and adolescents were enlisted into the struggle against Bolshevism. They were encouraged to send gifts to the front soldiers or support them in some other way. Although the youth organization's leadership knew very well that many of the front soldiers had been killed or injured, they painted a rosy picture of the struggle in the east. One example is a fabricated story from the publication *Nasjonal-Ungdommen*, which tells about a girl named Kari, who loved chocolate and was a member of the Småhird, the youth group for girls between ten and fourteen. The title was "Chocolate Is Good, but There Are Others Who Need It More than I Do."[14] The moral of the story was that everyone needed to make sacrifices for "our brave soldiers fighting out there on the front, who need encouragement more than we do." In this instance, Kari gave away her ration of chocolate. Eventually, packages full of chocolate from the Småhird girls reached "the boys in the bunker" who "had been on the frontlines for three days." Despite being "deathly tired," they could hardly contain themselves when the packages from Norway arrived. In this story, an eighteen-year-old named Jens received the chocolate along with a letter from Kari, which he held "tight in his fist" as he fell asleep that night. Later, Jens writes back to Kari that "this life is full of sacrifices, you know." Kari's chocolate was a sacrifice made "for the greater good," according to Jens, who firmly believed that he was fighting the good fight. He wrote that none of the volunteer front soldiers "regret that we signed up for this."

Around Christmas in 1942, the youth organization also published a book titled *Practical Handbook for the Gjentehird and the Småhird*. The Gjentehird was the organization for older girls, between fourteen and eighteen. This handbook provided detailed advice about sending packages to the Eastern Front and what they should include. Part of the advice was that "a Christmas letter and gift package mean even more for a soldier. A message from the home front lets them know about our unified will and our collective efforts. It is therefore an honor for each girl in the Hird to send at least one package to the front this year."[15] Petter, however, did not receive any chocolate or gift packages, and not very many letters either, in any case none from younger admirers. Thinking that Rolf had many female friends,

Petter earnestly requested the name and address of one of them. He really wanted a female pen pal, but he never found one.

Petter's characteristic defiance and fighting spirit slowly returned. Before he recovered and was able to walk again, he had already decided that he would continue to fight in the war even if he were given the chance to return to Norway permanently after the hospital visit. Despite the fatal errors in planning made by the German army leaders, he had no regrets about enlisting. "If duty calls," he wrote to Rolf, "then I will stay here and fight until the last battle is won."[16] He was afraid of being seen as a traitor to the cause, and he still held a passionate belief that it was necessary to wage war against communism. He asked Rolf what the mood was like in Raufoss: "Things have changed, I think. Have you joined the National Unification Party yet? You should soon. You're old enough now to understand the dangers our country was facing—and who was it who saved us? Quisling is the only answer." He hoped to see Rolf again and that this time both of them would be in uniform.

Petter disliked people who he thought were getting away with something or trying to milk the system at the expense of others. He noticed this at the hospital too; he was "tired of the Wehrmacht officers whining and moaning about their headaches while I was limping around without saying a word." True soldiers should not behave like that. Whining was a sign of weakness, which he despised. This was also one of the reasons why he wanted to return to the front, as he later explained: "That was when I started to think—should I really just keep lying here in bed? My comrades are out there fighting while I stay in here? I got obsessed with leaving the hospital, that's how I am, you know. So, the next day, I stopped the doctor on his morning rounds and told him I was ready to go back to the front."[17]

How did Petter manage to maintain his belief not only in the war but also in Vidkun Quisling? He was clearly motivated to keep going, no matter what happened. It seems that he had an almost religious sense of conviction, which sustained his spirit of defiance and sacrifice. His fanatical desire to stay the course is reminiscent of the fortitude of those on a polar expedition or a strenuous journey through the Himalayas or perhaps even a pilgrimage. Petter was being held captive, whether he knew it or not, and this entailed a peculiar form of loyalty and determination. Strong faith in the mission was needed to make it through alive, and those who doubted would perish. The war required soldiers, so if a soldier was prepared to make it to the front at any cost, no one was going to stop him. Petter found the nearest officer and declared himself ready for battle again. He would return to the front even if it killed him. He thought to himself that it wouldn't be right to stay at the hospital and "have a nice time" while his comrades fought hard in the war. As he later said, "It might have been that I thought it would be humiliating to go home. I didn't want to let anyone down. I wanted to do everything in the most honorable way possible. Dying on the field of honor, that was what I was thinking."

The ideals of honor and defiance in the face of struggle were also a central theme in the last letter Petter sent home to Rolf from the hospital: "When you receive this letter, I will be back where a soldier belongs—on the front. The Bolsheviks are attacking us day and night, but what's the use? They will be fought back wherever they are found, with thousands of casualties. It's a harsh battle in the snow and the cold, but we will stay strong. We know what is at stake: the freedom of Europe."[18]

At the hospital, he practiced walking in slippers and woolen socks, but when he was about to leave, he was given boots—which were a size too small. Petter forced them on. He was not only determined; he was reckless and took unnecessary risks. He received instructions to report to a staging area near a train station whose location he wasn't quite sure about. That was when he made a mistake. Too impatient to wait for the transport, even though his left foot was still far from healthy, he started to walk to the staging area. There was no way it could have gone well. Eventually, he had to face the music and head back to the hospital, where he stayed for one more night before finding a spot on a truck that was going out to the front.

Petter was now exactly where he wanted to be. On Easter Eve, March 16, 1942, he had again become a soldier in the service of Hitler in the war against the Bolsheviks. He could now load his rifle and put his helmet on. Just over two months after he had been rescued from freezing to death, he was back on the front again, joining in what he called "the fiercest battles." The Red Army continued its intense winter offensive, doing everything it could to win ground before the Germans had a chance to strike back.

Along with many other soldiers who had been injured or frostbitten in the winter, Petter came back just as the spring was arriving. However, he didn't see any of his former comrades, as he later explained: "There was such a lack of soldiers that they'd sent in new recruits. I went back to my old troop but didn't find anyone who'd been there before. My foot was still hurting, and I had problems keeping up."[19] Despite his injury, Petter had no plans of giving up; he would just forget about his foot. All soldiers who were injured in battle were supposed to be awarded a medal, called a wound badge. Petter did not receive one, because he never shed blood in battle, as was required. He had merely been frostbitten, and almost losing one of his legs was simply not good enough to be acknowledged with a medal.

CHAPTER 8

Honor and Allegiance

One day the winter suddenly ended. The German officers took note in their logbooks on March 25, 1942, when mild weather returned to the eastern front—along with a new round of endless mud and flooding that hindered any possible German offensive. There was no real spring; it just went straight from winter to summer, from frigid cold to heat.

As the first wartime winter on the eastern front was loosening its grip, Hitler was tightening his control over military planning and daily administration of the campaign. He had reduced the central military staff and assumed full authority. On April 5, Hitler announced his new plans for an ambitious summer offensive. Once again, he was convinced that his supremacy and strength would lead his troops to victory. The plans were formidable: Germany was going to attack along the entire front, but especially in the south. The troops were going to take Stalingrad, capture the oil fields in the Caucasus, and conquer all of Crimea, where the Red Army still held the major port city of Sevastopol.

First, however, Germany needed to regain lost positions. The Russians had secured several bridgeheads and moved forward over the winter; now they had to be driven back. Of particular importance was the oil. The previous plan had been to capture the oil fields both in the Caucasus and on the other side of mountains as early as October 1941, and it was supposed to take only a few weeks. Now, Hitler saw the fight for oil in a larger context: it was not just a matter of cutting off the Soviet oil supplies but of demolishing the Red Army's resistance. Hitler assumed that Stalin would redirect all his resources and reserves to protect the oil supplies. The

Germans would thus kill two birds with one stone, taking control of the oil and crushing the Soviet army at the same time.

~

Petter's left leg was still in pain, and he was still limping. He wrote to Rolf on April 23, 1942, "I'm not completely back to normal yet, and I'm not sure I ever will be, but things will work out." Petter no longer expected to return home anytime soon. At first, he thought he'd be home by Christmas, then Easter, then in the spring . . . Now, he didn't know anymore, and he wrote, "I think I'll be here until the very end."

In the letter, he continued to plead for support from his family at home, expressing anger and bitterness that they weren't on his side. He simply couldn't understand it—after he had sacrificed so much! Sure, he knew that his father would never support his decision, but what about Rolf? Did he not see that this was the right thing to do? Even though he knew his brother had joined Arbeidstjeneste, the labor agency of the occupation regime, which "was basically like the military," it still wasn't enough for him.

He complained again about receiving too few letters, explaining that Rolf should understand that he needed news from home. It was true that most of the letters he sent home probably vanished along the way, but still. He was jealous of his brother, who had taken a trip to the mountains for Easter, and he scolded him for taking a vacation when the war was much more important. "Can you imagine celebrating Easter in a dark bunker?" he asked, letting his resentment show. "Sure, you are all having a nice time. It's hard to think that we're here fighting for all these weaklings and cowards at home, and they just scoff and sneer at us. When we get home, we won't put up with much from them." The threats were not to be mistaken.

In Norway, the National Unification Party continued its antisemitic propaganda movement, which it connected to developments in the war. In the April edition of the monthly newsletter for party leaders, *NS Månedshefte*, one column stated, "Today, the powers of Jewry are fighting for their lives. The war has turned out to be different from what they expected."[1]

Three days after Petter wrote that he would stay "until the very end," whatever that meant, Hitler delivered one of his long speeches to the German Reichstag and attempted to explain what had gone wrong over the winter: "We were forced to fight against an unexpected enemy. The cold weather this year was the worst in 140 years. During Napoleon's campaign, the temperature did not go past 25 degrees below, but this year, it went down to 52 degrees below. . . . The enormous winter battle is now behind us. The time has come for the frozen fronts to be set in motion once again."[2]

The Red Army, however, was also planning a summer offensive to drive back the Germans. In the area around Kharkiv, where Petter was, the Soviets went on the attack on May 12. Their plan was to surround the German army units, but when the Germans began a counterattack only five days later, the Soviet troops were out of options. Within a week, as many as 240,000 Soviet soldiers had been taken captive. The Red Army had managed to mobilize a great number of new soldiers, but they weren't trained well enough, and many of them surrendered easily. The Germans found themselves with a large prisoner problem to sort out. Petter was put in charge of guarding prisoners, as he later recalled:

I remember being a prison guard clearly. There were around fifty to sixty Russians. We stared at each other, their many eyes against my two. Some of them slouched down on the ground, some stood and sent angry glances my way, but a few of them were tall, fair-skinned, with blond hair—like one of us—with an open gaze. It was hard to make them match the image of the enemy we had, but it was easier with the ones in the back, who weren't so nice looking, with their defiant, crooked eyes. Fascinating, but of course also depressing.[3]

Other Norwegians who encountered the Soviet prisoners were, like Petter, interested in their racial characteristics. A significant number of the soldiers in the Red Army were from the Asian parts of the Soviet Union, and they did not fit the image of how Norwegian Nazis thought people should look. Sigrun Nossum, the leader of the National Unification Party group for girls, visited the German-occupied areas along the Soviet border and was taken aback by how ugly the Russian prisoners were.

I also got to see Russian prisoners of war in a few prison camps. The pictures we have seen of the Bolshevik prisoners in the newspapers at home have certainly been dreadful, but to be honest, I think the Bolsheviks are even uglier in person. There was even a German guard who told me that the ugliest ones were not even present in the camps that I saw on this occasion.[4]

Lieutenant K. M. Opsahl of the Norwegian Legion, a collaborationist branch of the Waffen-SS, wrote the following after visiting a prison camp where he saw "tens of thousands of what one calls Russians." "After having seen these Asiatics, I find myself in complete agreement that they should never be allowed to reproduce. For me, it would not even help if they were to approach me with open arms; for the sake of our race and for the sake of our children, they must be eradicated, otherwise they will destroy all that is noble and pure."[5]

This hatred for the Russian "Asiatics" was brutal and racist. Hitler was also obsessed with the "barbarity of inner Asia."[6] Paradoxically, Germany had entered a formal alliance with Asia's great power, Japan. While Petter and the German troops were fighting tenaciously in the snow and cold, major events were taking place at much warmer latitudes. Early in the morning on December 7, 1941, Japan attacked the United States naval base at Pearl Harbor in Hawaii. Five American battleships, three cruisers, and four destroyers were sunk, and 188 airplanes were destroyed. Eighteen of the ninety warships at the base were either sunk or greatly damaged.[7]

On December 11, four days later, Germany declared war on the United States, thus acquiring yet another economic great power as an enemy.[8] Hitler put his trust in the fact that Japan had not lost a war in three thousand years, and he imagined that Japan and Germany together would be unbeatable.

Petter was glad that Japan had joined the war and described the Japanese as heroes. As he wrote in a letter to Rolf, he was looking forward to the "major German victories on the American coast and Japan's heroic battles in East Asia. There are certainly great things that even anti-Axis people have to admire." For Petter, the Japanese were obviously not Germanic or Nordic, but despite that, they would be useful in the fight against the United States and Great Britain.

～

Death was never far from Petter. Mere seconds or millimeters could make a difference. On one occasion, he was hit directly in the helmet, but, amazingly, the bullet barely reached the inner part of his helmet and failed to injure him. Another time, he dropped his pocket watch when he was standing guard in the trenches. As he bent over to pick it up, the two guards next to him were hit. They died instantly.

Death came for some and spared others at random. In July 1942, Petter heard the sad news that Reidar Seeberg of Regiment Germania had fallen. Reidar was reported missing on February 28, farther south in Ukraine, and it had become clear that there was no way he could have survived. In a letter to his brother Johan, Reidar mentioned that a friend from Gjøvik had been killed, adding that "the world must be unjust for him to be taken, he who has a home and parents, while I, who have neither, have been spared. It would have been better the other way around."[9] Reidar's turn would soon come. Bjørn Eide Sørlien, the third friend who enlisted with Petter and Reidar, made it through the first major battles but was killed in August 1943. Two other soldiers from Raufoss also fell in battle on the eastern front. Petter realized that the news of Reidar's death would make things even more difficult for his mother, who was in "a constant state of fear about finding out that something had happened to me. . . . I must say that I've been incredibly lucky."[10]

The death of Reidar Seeberg came as a shock to Petter. Reidar was a true friend, one of the very few that Petter had. He had not been prepared when they were separated into different regiments, but he never stopped believing they would meet again. Now his friend was gone. Death, the soldier's constant companion, had in a sense become habitual to Petter, and his ability to mourn had gradually faded away. Nonetheless, the day after he found out about Reidar, he was overtaken by rage and resentment. He wrote another letter to Rolf and, full of bitterness and anger, swore to avenge the deaths of Reidar Seeberg and Reidar Torp, another soldier from Raufoss.[11]

In May 1942, Quisling and the minister of justice, Sverre Riisnæs, visited the Norwegian volunteer soldiers in Ukraine. According to the newspaper coverage, Quisling passed out cigarettes, chocolate, and other treats to the "Norwegian boys" who he described as "true men and true warriors." For security reasons, the specific army unit and location that Quisling visited was never made public, but it is said to have been the village of Uspenka in the eastern Donbas. Petter did not get to meet the Norwegian leader. Quisling and his retinue also visited a village that was built according to "Germanic" principles. It was intended as a model village for propaganda purposes. The National Unification Party organ *Fritt Folk* reported that "all the dirt has been swept away, inside and outside. The Russians have been shown what Germanic civilization looks like." As Quisling concluded his visit to the village, which was called "U" in the newspaper article, an SS band played music by Edvard Grieg.[12] Quisling also had news to report when he returned to Norway; in a press meeting at Oslo's Grand Hotel on May 18, he stated that the Jewish people in the region he had visited were not being "treated brutally." As he explained, "They were marked with one white armband and a yellow spot on their backs, and of course they had to perform labor. But it is important to remember that the Jewish question there is a dreadful problem; after all, they have the world's greatest concentration of Jews."[13]

Petter continued to write letter after letter, his mood swinging from optimistic and belligerent conviction to resentment and anger over the fact that not everyone saw things as he did. These changes in his tone were also a reflection of how the war was going, although he did not include very many details about the fighting—that was not allowed. A letter to Rolf from June 15, 1942, expressed more interest in how the weather was shifting between rain and clear skies: "That's how it always is. The sky is always blue behind the clouds, as I like to think. Even though things can be pretty sad and lonely at times, I always look ahead to the day when the sun of peace will shine over Europe and our dear fatherland once more." Petter's letters were no longer signed "soldier" but rather "SS Schütze," or rifleman. The following month he moved up the military ladder to the rank of Sturmmann and received a pay raise.

~

When the summer was at its warmest, the war entered an even more frantic phase. The Germans were about to reach the goal of their offensive and head north toward Stalingrad and at the same time south into the Caucasus. On June 28, 1942, they started a major attack along the three-hundred-kilometer front. In ten days, the troops pushed two hundred kilometers to the east, crossed over the Don River, and retook the areas that the Red Army had previously driven them out of. The battles were intense and bloody, and Petter was part of this roaring advance. On July 20, he wrote to Rolf that it "gets so hot in the daytime that it's almost intolerable, but it usually cools down at night." The conditions were about to get even worse for the soldiers; they lacked water and food, and disease was rampant. The flies made thing worse, and malaria and dysentery became a huge problem. Starting at the end of July, the soldiers' rations would be halved in an effort to increase the food reserves for the winter.[14]

On July 23, Petter and the others in Regiment Nordland helped to retake the city of Rostov. After that, they were supposed to enter the Caucasus and take control of the oil fields near Maykop in the North Caucasus and Grozny in Chechnya. According to the German plan, they would also capture the more abundant oil fields near Tbilisi in Georgia and Baku in Azerbaijan, by the Caspian Sea. The Red Army had shown its strength, but the German troops had again tasted blood and were straining at the leash. Nothing would stop Germany when it really counted.

Petter was excited to see the Caucasus. He had read about the region in the book *In Wonderland* by his favorite writer, Knut Hamsun, which describes the author's journey to the region in 1899: "The smell of oil hangs over the entire city. It is everywhere, on the streets and in the houses." He also described his visit to the "black city" outside Baku, where all the oil refineries were.[15] This was the area the Germans wanted to conquer at any cost.

Petter never did get to follow in Hamsun's footsteps. He had a dramatic falling out with the German officers in his regiment, and about three months after he solemnly declared to his brother that he would stay in the war until the very end, he went home to Norway. He left foot was still not doing well, but the true reason he left was that he could no longer stand the rude and disrespectful tone of the officers. He thought that he deserved respect after returning to serve in the war even though he easily could have been placed on leave. His sense of honor was injured, and he thought it was unfair that the German officers would not treat the Norwegians as equals, like they deserved.

Petter's superiors, however, didn't want to let him slip away from service. On the contrary, they wanted him to attend the SS officer school in Bad

Tölz in Bavaria. He refused, which led to a bitter confrontation. Petter made it clear that he would prefer to go to the northern part of the eastern front, where Norwegian soldiers were needed. In the Norwegian Legion, there were many more Norwegians than in Regiment Nordland, and Petter wanted to be in an army unit made up of his own countrymen. Such requests only led to harsher rebukes from the officers, who suggested that Petter didn't think the Germans were good enough. Petter refused to give in, and at one point, the argument got so heated that he thought he might never make it home again. In the end, he got what he was hoping for. Regiment Nordland had no use for a volunteer soldier who couldn't stand being there. Petter said that he was being "released." He was upset but also happy to leave Ukraine, where he had witnessed so many evils of war. The war would need to move eastward without him.

Petter's fellow soldiers on the southern part of the front in Ukraine had been promised that they would get to wash their feet in the waters of the Caspian Sea, but there were many obstacles to be faced on the way. One of them was the Caucasian mountains, which stood like a stone wall of defense several thousand meters high. Crossing over these mountains involved going through narrow passes, which were guarded by specially trained sharpshooters. On August 9, 1942, German troops reached Krasnodar and Maykop, where they were disappointed to discover that the oil fields had been completely destroyed. The Germans who were attempting to reach Grozny in Chechnya didn't make it, because their trucks ran out of gas. The German offensive and its armored vehicles were stuck in the mountains. The distances were too great and the fuel too little.

On August 21, special forces from the First Mountain Division managed to plant the flag of Nazi Germany, with its swastika, at the summit of Mount Elbrus, the highest peak in Europe. This achievement had little significance except as propaganda, and not very much as that either. When Hitler was told that the soldiers had climbed all the way to the summit, he remarked joylessly, "Did they think they could outdo the Englishmen in terms of their athletic ambitions?"[16] Germany never did conquer the Caucasus.

While the Germans were directing resources to the southern flank, the Red Army was preparing for the next winter, while also assembling numerous forces for the decisive battle of Stalingrad that the Russians knew was to come. The Germans had few reserves left to draw from. With the summer offensive coming to an end, what mattered was to secure new positions before the arrival of winter.

The war was starting to look like a race against time for the Germans. On August 19, German forces began the attack on Stalingrad, but it was too late. The Red Army had rallied and regained its determination, while the Germans had overestimated their own strength and used up too many resources in the first phase of the summer offensive. The Russian watchword for the defense of Stalingrad was to "not give an inch," as the attackers would find out. The brutal conduct of the Germans had done little to weaken the Soviets' fighting spirit; rather, it had strengthened the entire population in its desire to fight back.

∿

Only a few days after fighting at the front, Petter was enjoying himself in Berlin. He left his division with a staff sergeant from the Wehrmacht, with whom he had previously had a heated argument, but that was all forgotten now. They arrived in Berlin and spent two days with "four bottles of schnapps. Two women. That was all, but it was plenty," as Petter wrote to Rolf on August 8. After his stay in Berlin, Petter had to work for a short time as a clothing manager at the officer school in Klagenfurt, Austria. The next stop was Hamburg and then home to Norway by train, first to Oslo and finally Raufoss.

It was a joy and a relief to come home. Petter was not afraid to show everyone who he was. In his SS uniform and his polished boots, tall and shiny, he arrived in Raufoss on August 27. He was a veteran, a soldier who had taken lives and seen his comrades die. He was proud of himself and expected to be received like a hero—had he not risked his life to defend Raufoss from communism?

Julie, his mother, was glad to see him again, but others in the family did not appreciate his German uniform. He had "made the whole family look like fools," and many people found it "embarrassing" that he went around showing off his uniform. As Rolf Westlie later said, "He just stood there in the kitchen in his uniform, looking all proud."[17] Petter, defiant as ever, was not willing to hide anything. He was disappointed—if only they had greeted him with a little more understanding, perhaps even some gratitude? Indifference was one thing, but some members of the family refused to even look at him. No, there was no way he could stay there. There were others who needed him more, much more than anyone at home. He told his mother, "I need to get out of here, I can't give up, even if I don't travel as far away this time." She was shocked that he was talking about going back into military service already. Enough was enough!

In every letter he had written home to his brother, Petter had expressed concern for his mother's health and well-being. He had a deep love for his mother. She meant more to him than anyone else; she was perhaps even the only one who mattered. Although he didn't always listen to everything she said, he looked up to her. For Julie, however, Petter was too stubborn; he was demanding too much from her, and the feelings of joy and relief about his return thus faded fast. He was trying to convince her to support his ideological endeavor. She had been hoping he was finished with the war and with Nazism, but he was far from it. They were both disappointed by each other. She did not understand how important the time at war had been to him. It was bad enough that his brother and father were hurtful to him, but for her to join them! From her he had expected understanding at the very least, maybe even praise for his efforts. But there was none. Petter's connection to his mother would never be like it was before 1940. They too had been torn apart by the war.

After only one day at home, he returned to Oslo to enlist for the second time. This time, he took the tram from the train station to the recruitment office, which had been moved from Parkveien to an even more elegant location at 105 Drammensveien. Petter arrived at the office to enlist in the SS Ski Jäger Battalion Norway, which was going to Finland. His plan was to turn in the SS Division Wiking uniform, change into a new uniform, and find out where he should report for their departure. He must have felt some doubt deep inside, even though he did not think much about it at first.

What happened next was something "wonderful," almost a "miracle."[18] During Petter's meeting with the Norwegian civil official at the office, a peculiar scene played out between the two men, one of whom wanted to enlist as a soldier and the other of whom was working to recruit soldiers.

"Are you really going to head out again?" asked the official, as he looked closely at Petter's papers and noticed that he had been hospitalized for frostbite injuries. He repeated the question.

"Yes, that's my plan," said Petter.

"You haven't frozen enough already?"

"Well, yes, but do I really have a choice?"

"Nothing in your papers says that you need to go back, so it's really up to you," said the official.

It was almost like the young official had seen through Petter, like he could see what Petter had been unwilling to admit. Was it Petter's doubt or simply that he was not entirely healthy?

Hearing those questions made Petter think again. If he went to serve again, he would have to endure at least one more wartime winter as a soldier. Would he be able to do that? Petter changed his mind right then and there. With relief, he withdrew his application and was discharged. The fact that it was a civil official, not a military one, and a Norwegian rather than a German must have made a big difference in the outcome of Petter's visit to the recruitment office that day.

Petter later said that it felt like he'd been sentenced to death and then pardoned. Six months after he left the front, the German army confronted the failures that it would never recover from. On January 31, 1943, General Friedrich Paulus surrendered, and thus the Wehrmacht's Sixth Army's attempt to capture Stalingrad ended in a pile of ruins and total defeat. The vanquished German soldiers were told by their Soviet counterparts that Berlin would end up looking like just like Stalingrad.[19]

Petter received news of the German failure to take Stalingrad with composure and mixed feelings.[20] He had learned firsthand, through the pain in his own body, that Hitler and his military leaders had misjudged the strength of the Soviet Union. Stalingrad was a tragic defeat for what Petter believed in, but he still did not give up. The nature of the war was changing for him, from an offensive attack abroad to defense at home. Petter wanted to take part in building a Norway led by the National Unificaton Party in collaboration with Nazi Germany.

PART II

CHAPTER 9

Punishment

"Do you really want to?" my father asked. He was pleasantly surprised when, in March 2004, I asked if he would sign an application to have his official sentence for treason released at the National Archives. I promised him that I would take care of the practical side.

After I received the sentence and read it, I immediately called to tell him about what it said. One of the parts I read aloud to him stated, "As a mitigating factor, the court has concluded that the accused cannot be said to have acted maliciously. He has explained himself clearly and directly to the court with apparent sincerity. As previously mentioned, he bitterly regrets what he has done, and he has indicated that he is finished with National Socialism forever."

"Does it really say that I didn't act maliciously?" He took a deep breath, but it was hard to tell if he was relieved or dejected.

"Yes, that's what it says here. How could the judge have known that?" I asked.

"I don't know, there must have been something."

"The sentence also says that you did not take an oath to Adolf Hitler when you joined Division Wiking, because you were sick. Was that right?"

"No, that part is not true. What nonsense! If you did not take the oath, they sent you home."

"There's also nothing in the sentence about your time as a soldier in Ukraine."

"That's because I was never asked or interrogated about anything from that time. None of the people who interrogated me were interested in anything I did in Ukraine or what happened there."

When my father read his sentence for the first time, at the age of eighty-five, he wrote notes in the margins and marked certain parts of the text with exclamation points and questions. During our conversations, it became clear to me that there were many things he hadn't told them during the sentencing, which they didn't ask about either. For example, the fact that he had been a member of Germanic SS Norway is not even mentioned in the sentence. Whoever investigated his case did not take a close enough look at his activities during the war, and he had done what he could to keep them from finding out about everything. "The important thing was to minimize what I had done."[1]

~

Petter scoffed at the indictment when at 10:45 a.m. on April 30, 1946, the police officer R. Hagen read it aloud to him in his cell in Oslo Prison, Department B. He had been arrested on May 14 the previous year, and then he had waited and waited, facing what he described as "starvation and harassment."[2] After the indictment was finally prepared, things moved quickly. The trial took place on June 24, and a guilty verdict was handed down immediately along with a sentence: three years and four months of forced labor, with a deduction of 407 days spent in custody. As additional punishment, Petter lost his rights as citizen for ten years, which meant that he was not allowed to vote in any elections—even if he had wanted to.

Petter didn't get to read the sentence for treason. It was read to him, but he could hardly hear it. The basis for his punishment was "the standard criminal code of May 22, 1902, section 86, cf. the provisional ordinance of October 3, 1941, regarding the addition to that law, and the provisional ordinance of December 15, 1944, regarding the addition to the criminal legislation on treason (the treason ordinance), section 51," which states that "these decisions set the punishment for those who unlawfully bear arms against Norway, or who, during a war in which Norway is participating, or with such a war in mind, provide assistance to the enemy in counsel or deed, or weaken the combat capability of Norway or any state in alliance with Norway."[3] The fact that Petter's immediate family members never joined the National Unification Party was seen as an aggravating factor. Petter could not "resort to the argument that he came from a Nazi home."

They can do whatever they want, he thought. But the sentence still hit hard, not because he had a guilty conscience but because he despised the court and the judgment of the victors. Real justice was impossible, he thought. In any case, he was still convinced that he had done the right thing for Norway. As he wrote, "I was a participant in 'the great drama' of the legal purge that started in the spring of 1945, which was harsh and ruthless to the thousands of kind-hearted Norwegians who had been working day and night throughout the long war years to make things as painless as possible for our countrymen, both the good and the bad ones."[4] In other words, the part of the sentence that says he felt regret was greatly exaggerated.

He was one of 4,272 Norwegian war volunteers who were sentenced for having provided "armed assistance to the enemy." The average punishment for those who had enlisted in the German army—who had "only" done that and nothing more—was around three years and four months. Petter's sentence was thus in line with that of others, although he didn't serve the entire punishment.

When Petter was discharged from the army in August 1942, he decided to go into the Germanic SS Norway, a paramilitary organization that had been established in July the same year. It was like going to serve on the front but at home in Norway.[5] Front soldiers were strongly encouraged to join the organization after completing their military service; some of them apparently felt forced to do so. Petter had heard about its founding while he was still in Ukraine. He noted in a letter home that it sounded like something for him.

The Germanic SS Norway was a minor offshoot of the Germanic SS in Germany, which itself was a subsection of the SS, as was the Waffen-SS. The goal of the group was to work toward establishing the Greater Germanic Reich, and it was much more pro-German, more extreme in its Nazi views, and more race oriented than the National Unification Party. The intended task of the organization was to be a "powerful, battle-ready reserve force for the hard times that may lie ahead."[6] Many front soldiers wanted to use their war experience to fight against the "inner" enemies in Norway. In a letter home from the front, one soldier wrote, "We will be tough guys when we come home in one or two or four years, and we won't be afraid to face any 'resistance' from those soft mama's boys and chatterboxes."[7]

The extremely pro-German minister of police, Jonas Lie, was the head of the Germanic SS Norway and was thus in this capacity subject to the authority of Reichsführer Heinrich Himmler, not Quisling. Along with Lie, two other collaborationist ministers were also members of the organization, which didn't exactly please Quisling.[8] The Germanic SS Norway wanted to "create a healthy nation of people with unimpeachable goals, a nation of people who want to defend the family and who understand the significance of selective breeding."[9] In addition, "as the representative of one of Europe's most racially pure peoples," it wanted "the preservation of our pure race." This was to be achieved through a "National Socialist revolution" in Norway."[10]

The Norwegians in the organization wanted to scare people and impress them in equal measure—uniforms, parades, and masculinity were all important to them. The troops would march in lockstep. "The sight of black columns of soldiers marching fills our hearts with joy," an observer wrote about the annual "SS Day" celebration, when members practiced their war skills. "Hand grenade throwing is a worthy and useful sport," it added.[11]

In September 1942, Petter was at the fortress in Kongsvinger, where recruits in the Germanic SS Norway received their instruction. Some of the German police battalions who had taken part in battles and carried out attacks on the eastern front also received further training in Kongsvinger.[12] It is possible that some of them were there at the same time as Petter, when the recruits took a four-week course in politics and ideology with an emphasis on racial doctrine. The course included eleven lectures the students were required to attend with titles such as "The Scientific Basis of the National Socialist Worldview," "Freemasonry as a Tool of Jewry," "The Idea of Order and Community in the National Unification Party," "The Basic Tenets of Heredity," and, of course, "The Jews." The lecture on the Jewish people described Hitler's contribution as follows: "Then the führer seized victory from their hands and pushed aside the seducers of the people. Many of the worst Jews were confined and forced to work in concentration camps."[13] It concluded, "each and every SS man must know this: Jewry and the Jewish spirit have always been the archenemy of Nordic blood. . . . When we remove the Jews from our body of people, it will be an act of self-defense."

Petter was proud to participate in the course in Kongsvinger, writing "All is well!" to Rolf and signing the letter "Heil og Sæl!"—the version of the

Old Norse greeting used by the National Unification Party.[14] His uniform was decorated with the party's symbol, the sun cross, and a raven. He was looking forward to the military parade the Germanic SS Norway was planning in Oslo. The organization was going on the offensive on several fronts. For a long time, both the Germanic SS Norway and the National Unification Party had inflamed antisemitic sentiment and indirectly incited violence. For them, the battle was far from over, as much work remained to be done to nazify Norway. Part of this work was getting rid of the Jews, a task that the Germanic SS Norway was eager to accomplish. As attacks on the Norwegian Jews escalated in the fall of 1942, the organization's magazine, *Germaneren*, added fuel to the fire. The lead article of its October issue emphasized that the era when Jews lived in Norway would soon be over: "Today the country is being cleansed of the Jewish influence. The Germanic SS Norway will act as a guarantee that the Jews and their pawns will never again bring misfortune to the Norwegian people."[15]

In the same issue, a new law was announced: "Jewish assets will be confiscated for the benefit of the state treasury." In the National Unification Party Yearbook for 1942, this was presented as one of the party's most important "accomplishments" that year. The plundering of the Norwegian Jews' property was one of several steps on the road to the catastrophe that would come.

The actions against the Jews were carried out in several distinct phases, beginning in Trondheim on October 6 and 7 and then spreading to the rest of the country. On October 26, 336 Jewish men, mainly in southern Norway, were arrested at their homes by Norwegian police and other officials and sent to the prison camp Berg outside Tønsberg. Twenty-eight members of the Germanic SS Norway took part in the arrests in Oslo; they were requisitioned on orders from the state chief of police.[16] They each received twenty kroner as "reimbursement" for the arrest of "Jews to be secured." As they were taught at the fortress in Kongsvinger, removing the Jews was considered a form of "self-defense." Available evidence suggests that Petter was in Oslo when this occurred, though he did not take part in the arrests. His name is not on the list of participants from the organization.

On November 25 and 26, officials rounded up Jewish women, children, and the elderly in Oslo and surrounding areas, again with the help of participants from the Germanic SS Norway.[17] With the aid of around a hundred taxis, the Jewish people were brought to the Oslo harbor, where the

transport ship *Donau* was waiting. On the ship, they were stowed together
with people who had been arrested earlier. The ship sailed to Szczecin in
Poland with a cargo of 532 Jews: 302 men, 188 women, and 42 children.[18]
They were then sent to Auschwitz. More Jewish people would later follow
by ship from Oslo harbor. Any lists that may have existed of the men from
the organization who participated in the final round of arrests have not
been found.

~

I was relieved to discover in the summer of 2007 that my father had not
taken part in the arrests of November 1942. However, a somewhat self-
centered thought also occurred to me. If he had been involved in the
arrests, it would have meant that I was right to have shunned him for all
that time. I would have had the upper hand, morally speaking, especially
since I had written articles and a book about the economic consequences
of the anti-Jewish actions in occupied Norway.[19] When I came to my senses,
though, all my doubts were gone, and I was relieved to know that my father
had not been directly involved in the arrests.

And yet he must have known what was happening when the Jews were
detained and deported, and he remained a member of the Germanic SS
Norway even after the deportations took place. Couldn't he have left the
organization? Was there a possibility of punishment if he did so? Had he
already seen and done too much to turn back? Or perhaps he was simply
not very concerned by the fact that Jewish people were being brutally deported from Norway. Was he still afraid of being seen as a turncoat?

In Petter's postwar trial for treason, one of the aggravating factors was that
he had "made no attempt to leave" the National Unification Party. As he
noted in a comment on the court papers, trying to escape to Sweden would
have been in vain, an "idiotic idea." Party members who fled to Sweden
were at risk of being sent back to Oslo, because the Swedes would not
accept them. If that happened, "you were really on thin ice." According to
Petter, he was too closely connected to the Nazi regime in Norway to leave.
Both the National Unification Party and the Germanic SS Norway were
totalitarian groups with strict internal discipline. Breaking away would have
been seen as traitorous, and he would have lost his friends and his community. Who else did he have? He was more or less estranged from his family
and no longer felt at home in Raufoss. Of course, this cannot explain why

he took part in the war against the Soviet Union in the first place and even less so why he remained an active supporter of a regime that arrested and deported Jewish people from the country.

~

The Germanic SS Norway was in effect a German "cell" within the organizational structure of the National Unification Party, and this attracted criticism from some party members. It was seen as "specialized agency" within the party, which meant it was outside of the party's control.[20] The organization consisted of around 1,200 men and was clearly in competition with the Hird, the party's paramilitary guard. In theory, members of the Germanic SS Norway were not allowed to be part of the Hird at the same time. It did occur in practice, however, which heightened tensions within the party, as the Germanic SS Norway was based on pan-Germanic rather than Norwegian nationalist ideals.

In 1943, Petter was an active member of the Germanic SS Norway, on duty in the area between Raufoss and Oslo as a guard and participant at various events. On August 15, 1943, he was promoted to the rank of SS Sturmmann. He was also a squad leader of the Vestre Toten branch of the Hird.[21] This was not entirely unproblematic. At the same time, he was also the leader of the National Unification Party's youth organization in Vestre Toten.[22] By his own account, all he did in that role was lead a few meetings in which he shared his war experiences and answered questions from younger party members.

While Petter was moving back and forth between Oslo and Raufoss in June 1943, a German officer was found dead on the street in the center of Raufoss. To force a confession, two hostages were taken from Raufoss, a popular doctor and a former local politician. The situation was tense, and the Germans were deadly serious: if the case was not cleared up by July 1, the hostages would be shot. At the last minute, it became clear that the officer had been shot by another German in a crime of passion. The hostages were released, but the incident had shown that the Germans would not refrain from using violence in Raufoss, a place where they had been cautious so as to ensure the continued production of weapons.[23]

As Christmas 1943 approached, Petter began a six-month training course at the Police Academy in Oslo. The leaders of the police force wanted to incorporate former front soldiers, who were given preference as applicants.

All aspects of policing in Norway were going to be nazified. The Germans and their supporters wanted to turn Norway into a police state and would stop at nothing to make that happen.

The background of Petter's decision to join the police force was dramatic. On August 16, 1943, the German intelligence agency, Sicherheitsdienst, and the Gestapo arrested 470 employees at various levels within the police force. On the same day, the police officer Gunnar Eilifsen was executed for disobedience after declining to arrest five young women who had refused to report for forced labor. In December, the arrested police officers were sent to Stuffhof, a concentration camp in Poland.[24] This action against the police, which had the code name Arctic Circle, came after the Germans and their Norwegian collaborators had conducted a review of the "reliability" of the police force. The ones who were arrested had been characterized as unreliable, even though 42 percent of the police officers who were employed before 1940 had in fact joined the National Unification Party after an aggressive recruitment campaign soon after the party took power.[25] It was in this situation, with several hundred police officers behind bars, that Petter decided to join the force. Men like him were intended to replace the men who had been arrested.

In the fall of 1943, Petter lived in a boarding house on Uranienborgveien in Oslo; after Christmas, he moved to the Landåsen Hotel in Søndre Land, near Gjøvik, "to continue his training," as he wrote in a letter.[26] He also mentioned that he would continue to serve in the "old storm," in a subsection of the Germanic SS Norway, until further notice. Petter's decision to join the police may have been a way to escape into a civilian profession, as he hinted in a written note, but it is impossible to say for sure.

On April 17, 1944, Petter became a police detective in Oslo, having passed the investigator course with a grade of "highly satisfactory." After a training period that included eighty-five hours of "forensic science," seventy hours of "boxing and police actions" and ninety hours of "gymnastics and exercises," he was ready to enforce law and order. But he would only stay in this position for about a year. The end of the war was coming, and the tide was turning against the Germans more and more every day. The Red Army was picking up speed in the east, while British and Americans troops were approaching from the south and the west.

At the time Petter joined the police, desperation had already begun to spread among Norwegian Nazis. Many of them sensed the danger. The lead article in the March 1944 issue of the magazine *Austrvegr* asked, "Are there many people wavering now, not daring to stay the course out of fear of what will happen if the front abroad collapses?" "It is normal," the author noted, "to ask such questions when one thinks of the homeland every day. But if we on the home front fail to withstand the pressure, it would be a slap in the face to the men who are risking their lives abroad."[27] The author then added, perhaps to console himself as much as his readers, that the fight was about something much greater: "Our outlook does not depend on the changing course of the war. It is dictated only by the greatness of the cause itself." What was even greater than the war? Honor?

Petter's responsibility as a police detective, working at the city's main station at Møllergata 19, was to investigate criminal offenses, but he also helped investigate acts of sabotage. In his sentence for treason, it says that he only "performed ordinary police work and did not participate in political activities" and that there was no evidence to indicate that he was "involved with anything other than purely criminal cases." However, it is not so easy to distinguish what the Norwegian police did from what the German security police did. There was no clear line between the civilian police and the political police. Petter remained a member of the Germanic SS Norway, even wearing his SS uniform on the job at times, although it is not clear how often he did so or on what occasions.[28]

Petter felt caught between a rock and hard place. He was supposed to find and arrest criminals, but criminality is not a neutral concept. Robbing a bank, for example, might be a political act if the money is going to be used in the resistance, and it is not necessarily terrorism to attack military targets when the country is occupied. Norwegian resistance groups carried out daring assassinations right under the noses of the Norwegian police and the German military. In 2005, Petter recalled in a note that "as new officers, we were often sent out on new assignments in the almost pitch-black city."[29] He claimed that the senior officers at the police station understood "that we were not unbearable 'Nazis' but rather ordinary, hardworking compatriots who yearned to do something for the country, which was in an increasingly anxiety-provoking, 'war-like' situation, with arsons and explosions that many of us saw as pointless. You often asked yourself who was an enemy and who was a friend."

On May 19, 1944, the resistance hero Gunnar Sønsteby took part in the bombing of the Arbeidstjeneste (labor agency) office in the center of Oslo. It was such a daring operation that Petter and his police colleagues couldn't help but admire the courage and skill of the resistance members. After Sønsteby managed to swipe archival documents from the Ministry of Justice from right under the Germans' noses, the police said to each other, "They just got a hold of everything on us."

Four months after Petter started working as a police detective, he married Agnes, the woman who would become my mother. They had already lived together for a while in a "maid's room" on Drammensveien. Now that they were going to be proper spouses, they moved to a small apartment on Bygdøy allé. One of Petter's police colleagues served as his marriage witness, while one of Agnes's friends, a waitress, was hers. They could have been given a better place to live after they got married. The National Unification Party authorities managed the apartments of Norwegians who had either fled the country or been sent to prison camps in Norway or abroad. Such apartments were often given to returning soldiers from the eastern front or to party officials. However, my father claimed that he didn't want to live in that sort of apartment and not in one that had belonged to Norwegian Jews either: "Why did I not take advantage of the opportunities that existed during the war? I wouldn't have been able to look my neighbors in the eyes if I had done something morally questionable like that." Although he didn't accept an apartment, he was given a dinner set and silverware from the authorities when he got married. These were taken from confiscated apartments.

Agnes took care of the home while Petter was at work. Every morning, after he left, she would turn around the portrait of Quisling that he had hung on the wall. In addition to being opposed to Quisling, Agnes was against Nazism in general. Although she did marry Petter, she feared what the future with him might bring. It was obvious to her that Petter had bet on the wrong side and done bad things. That was why their first Christmas as a married couple, in 1944, was to be the last one for many years.

Petter grew more afraid of defeat and the potential postwar consequences, as can be seen in the few letters he wrote to Rolf near the start of 1945. But he also tried to trivialize the situation. On January 19, 1945, he wrote that "nothing has been bombed since New Year's Eve, so it's all just rumors. There is peace and quiet in the city now, sometimes an air-raid siren, but no one really cares about that." A few months later, the situation had become truly dire; all was lost for the National Unification Party regime and the German occupiers. Petter wanted to sort things out, repay what he owed his siblings, and get rid of things he no longer needed or wanted. He had to save whatever could be saved. On May 3, he wrote to Rolf:

> Rolf, would you please pack up all my things that are still at home and send them to me in a package? Some of it can also be burned. You can figure out for yourself what to send and what to destroy, right? I would have come home to visit and talk about it with all of you, but there won't be time for that. You must tell Mom that she doesn't need to be afraid for me, everything will go as it is destined.

He also asked Rolf to sell him a raincoat, since Agnes didn't have one and "couldn't go outside when it rains." Rolf never sent the raincoat, but he did get rid of many of the things Petter had kept in their childhood home—letters, uniforms, and other materials that detailed Petter's time as a front soldier and SS officer. It was time to eliminate the evidence.

What did Petter mean when he wrote that it was "destined" that things would turn out as they did? These days in May 1945 were indeed a fateful time, but did he mean that fate would decide what happened? Or did he believe that Hitler's Germany had already sown the seed of its own destruction when it embarked on war?

～

The end had come for the Third Reich. Hitler had taken his own life. Time was up for the Norwegians who had seized power when the Germans offered it with guns and tanks. It was all over within a matter of days after Petter sent his last letter to Rolf. Petter and the other collaborators were suddenly criminals. His past had caught up with him, but he refused to accept the reality. Was he being naïve or simply defiant? On May 8, 1945 (Victory in Europe Day), Petter went to work as usual, as if nothing had happened, and signed in for his shift at the police station at Møllergata 19.

He knew perfectly well what was going on; it had been clear since May 2 that Berlin had fallen, and whatever was left of German resistance was about to vanish completely. Germany had unconditionally surrendered to the Allies on May 7, and yet Petter went to his regular job the next day. This act was not only defiant but reckless. During the night of May 7 and into the morning of May 8, it looked as if the battle would continue at Møllergata 19. There were rumors that the minister of police, Jonas Lie, and his loyal supporters, many of them former eastern front soldiers, were planning to occupy the building. This led Milorg, the military resistance organization, to erect barricades and wooden barriers in the streets around Møllergata 19, so that it could confront Nazis who were unwilling to give up the fight. Armed police officers who were part of the resistance movement were also going to help defend the building. But Lie and his followers never showed up.[30] Petter, however, came to work like it was an ordinary day on the job.

His workday didn't last long. First, his supervisors, two senior officers, were arrested. Right after that, Petter was told that he could either go home or remain at the station until further notice. To judge from one of his cassette recordings, it appears that he was overwhelmed with emotion:

I felt like a page torn out of a book, like I was being taken out of context as I quietly left the station, full of the strangest conflicting emotions. A painful kind of sadness—I must have known that I was walking down that long hallway for the last time, where I frequently, or in any case many times, had walked in with a feeling of triumph to transcribe an oral confession I had obtained. Now it was over and done. In retrospect, I've wondered, was it all in vain? I'll never get an answer to that. And everything was different starting when I got there that morning. . . . It wasn't at all like it had been before. Suddenly, the heroes showed up in the hallways with their British Sten guns. They sat in the offices and smoked cigarettes. It was surprising to see who some of them were—oh, so you weren't in the National Unification Party after all, I thought. But most of them were cheerful, one even winked at me; he had a Sten gun on each shoulder. Maybe they thought I was a double agent, that did happen sometimes. I won't complain about being treated poorly that day because I wasn't. They couldn't possibly have believed . . . that I felt very guilty when I gave myself up. Yeah, well, I'm a bit naïve, but

I was stubborn, I must admit. I was right in the middle of an investigation that I thought I was about to solve. It was ridiculous. But I took my police work very seriously.

Petter walked out of the building onto the street. He wasn't a prisoner, but he wasn't free either. He was twenty-five years old and had no idea what the rest of his life would bring. It felt like "the building guards were staring directly at him." On the way home to his apartment on Bygdøy allé, there were Norwegian flags everywhere, and everyone was shouting "We are free!" while he thought to himself, "All is lost." What was going to happen to him now? How would Agnes take the news? Would she return to her family in Gjøvik? Would they even be willing to take her back?

Thoughts were swirling in his head: should he turn himself in, hide, or try to escape? He needed time to think, and he had an option: Trygve Skullerud's apartment at Brugata 7 in the center of Oslo. Skullerud, a furrier, had given Petter the key and asked him to check in on the apartment. A few days earlier, his store had been broken into and a large sum of money stolen. Petter's investigation hadn't led to anything, and Skullerud fled the city, thinking that he might be a target. He claimed that the resistance movement had threatened to shut him down because he had made a fortune selling furs to the Germans. Now Petter had an apartment to use as a place to lie low. He picked up Agnes and went to the apartment, where they met some friends, other people who needed to figure out what they were going to do. As Petter later explained in a cassette recording,

We all had something to drink and tried to think through the situation. We tried to console each other. I especially remember three of the people who were there: Andreas Sætrang, who was quite disheveled, the college student Per Samuelsen, and the fair-haired Viking Stein Sørensen—and of course your mother. Plus a few other women. We spent the first day almost like voluntary prisoners. I recall that we heard gunshots, and the mood was tense. I left the apartment, I can't remember if I went alone, but in any case, I went for a walk on Karl Johan and along Torggata Street. I was getting a bit emotional about not being able to participate in all the joy at the war being over, at least here in Europe. I went back inside pretty quickly; I was too afraid of being recognized.

They ended up leaving the apartment; Agnes headed home to Bygdøy allé, while Petter went with Stein to his house.

> But the soldiers showed up within fifteen minutes. There were around seven
> or eight of them, and they said that it was time for us devils to be taken away.
> Stein was their main target. I just sat there, and no one seemed to care much
> about me. But then I told them that I was cut from the same cloth, and they
> arrested me too. We sat in the police van, I had a chance to get some under-
> wear—and I also got to say goodbye to Agnes.

Petter, along with many other prisoners, was taken to what had been the wartime prison camp Grini in Bærum, outside Oslo, which was now known as Ilebu (later changed to Ila Prison). He was only at Ilebu for a brief time before being sent to Oslo Prison on Åkebergveien. The very first time Agnes came to visit, he told her that he wanted a divorce. At best, he thought he would be imprisoned for many years, and he couldn't stand to think about "her being out there while I was on the inside." In the worst-case scenario, he feared that he and the other eastern front volunteers would be executed. Agnes refused to leave him; she had chosen him and wanted to stick to-gether, despite everything. It was not an easy decision. If she had chosen a divorce, everyone, including her family, would have understood and sup-ported her. Divorcing Petter also could have been a way to make amends for having been foolish enough to marry someone like him in the first place. She was only eighteen and lonesome when she had made the decision. By staying at his side, the sentence and punishment he faced would also be hers.

Petter's life was transformed during his time in prison; that was when a "bitterness took hold in me" that never "loosen its grip."[31] Agnes's life was changed just as much by Petter's time behind bars. She had no money, but she eventually found a job at a factory that made blankets and pillows and a place to live in a tiny room in a villa on Kirkeveien in Oslo. She would be able to cope with the situation until Petter was released.

Petter spent a total of 417 days in prison in Ilebu and Oslo Prison, but in later years he was reluctant to say anything about that time. There is no doubt that he and his fellow inmates received harsh and brutal treatment. Both the press and public opinion were against those who had joined forces with the enemy. Various sources reveal that many of them were subject to physical and psychological abuse.[32]

Agnes was Petter's contact with the outside world, and she would stand outside the prison walls as often as twice a week hoping to talk with him if he was standing at a window. If she was lucky, he would look back through the iron bars, and they would wave to each other. In this too, she was taking a risk. Standing outside the prison was hard. People walking by understood what sort of prisoner she was there to see, and sometimes she heard them shout "Traitor!" But she gritted her teeth, since she knew it wasn't true, at least not about her.

While Agnes tried as hard as she could to arrange her life alone, Petter read everything he could get from the prison library, from textbooks to novels. He wanted to acquire knowledge, so that when he was released, he would be able to support himself and get a job. He didn't know whether he would have to start school over again or if he would be able to study at a university. He didn't know anything about what would happen, except that he should read as much as possible.

In Petter's prison cell, there were several others in his exact situation. The prison was full of people waiting to hear their sentences for treason: "Month after month, we shared the cell—five to seven of us, at least—with a sink, a toilet, mattresses on the floor. We took turns sleeping, if we got any sleep at all! No visits, all our mail was checked."[33] The defeat of Germany on May 8, 1945, had led to mass arrests of National Unification Party members and collaborators. Fourteen thousand people had already been arrested by July 1, which meant that two hundred temporary prisons and labor camps needed to be established. On August 6, 1946, as prisoner 164, Petter was relocated from Oslo Prison to the Bjørkelangen labor camp in the municipality of Nordre Høland in Akershus County.[34] It was even harder for Agnes to visit him there.

For Petter, it was a relief to be taken to Bjørkelangen after the long days he spent in Oslo Prison. He would remain there for one year and five days, but he was no longer confined behind walls or fences, and there were no guard dogs or armed prison guards keeping an eye on him. In fact, it was quite possible to run away, but Petter didn't do so. He knew he had to get through this punishment.

The camp at Bjørkelangen had been established in 1941 to house the National Unification Party labor agency, and it later became a training center for soldiers on their way to the eastern front. In February 1946, it was reopened for use as a labor camp for people serving treason sentences. Bjørkelangen had 181 prisoners at its height, including informers and torturers. Sixteen of them had initially been sentenced to death but then pardoned.[35] Many of the prisoners had been eastern front soldiers like Petter.

One question the authorities needed to address after the liberation of Norway was how to treat the prisoners, who had different backgrounds and had been sentenced for different crimes. A committee appointed in 1945 stated in a report, "the most important objective in the treatment of prisoners is . . . to preserve their ability to work, their physical health, and their mental well-being, so that after their punishment is served it will be possible once again for them to be productive and useful members of society."[36] But was it enough to simply let the prisoners work? Would that turn them into opponents of Nazism? Even if not, it was nevertheless not clear that it would be right to give political lessons to the prisoners. The commission argued, "The prisoners are suspicious and on guard against anything resembling propaganda, and they are steadfast in their earlier convictions. . . . Any ideological influence should therefore appear to be as little like propaganda as possible. It should certainly not seem to be something intended only for traitors but rather a part of the general instruction given to everyone."

Since the prisoners weren't offered any special programs or therapy of any sort, the guards and the supervisors didn't talk to them about their war experiences—that was not allowed. The prisoners at Bjørkelangen had a large amount of freedom; they weren't confined, they could subscribe to newspapers and magazines, and the mail wasn't censored. As a former guard said, "They were supposed to atone by working, but in practice there was no rehabilitation."[37] The prisoners were allowed to receive visits from family members. Wives or girlfriends also visited during "unregulated" time.

Petter worked as a lumberjack and rebuilt his strength and the muscle he had lost while in prison in Oslo. He was eating enough food, and he even claimed that the prisoners received more food of higher quality than most people in the immediate postwar years. They did need a lot of food, as they were being forced to work hard for the country they had betrayed. In addition to felling timber, Petter helped build roads through the forest for landowners and farmers, and he helped drain a nearby lake. Since he had experience with physical labor from before the war, he was more accustomed to it than many of the other prisoners. There were many requests to use the camp prisoners as manpower, but the supervisors refused to hire them out more than four kilometers away from Bjørkelangen.[38]

Petter started to dream of a life outside Norway, learning languages in his free time, including French and a bit of Spanish. More than a few of the prisoners were well educated and able to teach languages to others. Many of the people serving treason sentences planned to flee to South America. In July 1947, the ship *Solbris* left Askøy, near Bergen, for Latin America, with Argentina as its final destination. On board were eleven people who were serving treason sentences. Four of them had managed to escape from the prison camp near Espeland. They reached Brazil at the end of August, and the Norwegian authorities tried to have them extradited. The Brazilian supreme court, however, declared them political refugees and refused Norway's demands. The *Solbris* was not the only ship with refugees that took off from Norway; a total of twelve ships were said to have transported Norwegian traitors out of the country. The last one, *Ida II*, arrived in Argentina in January 1950.[39] Little is known about what sort of life they led once they got there.

Petter also considered fleeing the country, though nothing came of it. Agnes wanted to stay in Norway, and Petter had doubts about the idea of leaving. Where would he go? Wasn't it just as easy to pay his debt to society and get it over with? Fleeing to another country would have felt like abandoning Norway.[40]

The labor camps for the traitors became hotbeds of die-hard Nazis, who set up their own regime of internal justice and discipline. No one who had belonged to their war community would simply break away. It turned out to be difficult to escape from such a life of inner exile. The brotherhood of former National Unification Party members persists among the few who are still living and still zealous about their war experiences. The author Egil Ulateig, who for many years was in close contact and even friendly with some of these men, has described the situation:

> It was as if the punishment, the hatred, and the condemnation from the outside world only brought them closer together. Some of them admitted

that they first felt "saved" while in prison or in a labor camp. It was like the war had entered a new phase for them. They refused to accept any blame for what they had done and formed a lifelong network of devotees, kept alive by frequent meetings of comrades with toasts and speeches and those loud, pompous SS march songs.[41]

Professor of jurisprudence Johannes Andenæs researched the "resocialization" of the Norwegians who served treason sentences, and he argued that an attempt at political reeducation would have only made the problem worse. The prisoners were basically immune to counterarguments: "A common observation was that most of the prisoners were willing to acknowledge their mistakes immediately after the liberation but that this mood would often be replaced later by a bitter and aggressive attitude. Anyone who admitted his guilt in court would have to face being frozen out by the other prisoners when he came to the camp."[42] Few, if any, gave up without a fight in court, and neither did Petter, although he did not join the brotherhood of comrades established by the former front soldiers. He remained on the outside and only had occasional contact with the group. Instead, he tried to suppress his experiences in prison and at Bjørkelangen. That entire period was like a black hole in his mind. Being imprisoned was an experience of unending degradation for him.

~

Petter was released from Bjørkelangen on September 2, 1947.[43] Six years and eight months after he had taken the train from Raufoss to enlist, he was once again on a train to Oslo to start a new life. There were 355 days left in his prison sentence, almost a full year, but he was let out early on probation. He and Agnes were reunited in Oslo and intended to move on with their lives together if possible. Something was broken for him, but not for her, and she would do everything in her power to help Petter and save their marriage. Less than two years later, they had two sons, although only one of them reached adulthood, and several years after that, they had a daughter.

My father had been given back his freedom, but he was not at peace. He went into an inner exile, taking the family with him. Survival was necessary, but he simply would not compromise. What mattered most was providing for the family, and he got a job and worked hard. While others with a similar background used their friends and acquaintances to move onward and upward, he refused to do so. Although he was skilled at many things, he remained a defiant loner. Decades later, in one of the cassette recordings, he told me what life in the postwar years had been like for him.

> In my desperate situation, I felt no need to reveal anything, and no one had to know anything about me, so I managed to struggle through—I'm not sure whether you've understood that. I could have done much more in life if not for this heavy burden on my shoulders. I didn't want to show anyone who I really was. I know there were others like me who did—and many of them were also accepted—but I didn't want to.

His bitter feelings about the defeat and his conviction lingered on. My father hid his sorrow deep inside, and it never went away.

CHAPTER 10

Fear

The first thing I noticed when I finally opened the eight tightly packed cardboard boxes full of newspaper clippings and documents that my father had left behind when he moved away from Oslo in 2005 were the crosses. On newspaper photos, he had drawn crosses on the faces of politicians, academics, or anyone else he deemed too pro-immigrant. It was his own voodoo ritual, like he was branding them to make them disappear. He had clipped article after article from many different newspapers and added caustic and hateful comments. The people with crosses drawn on their foreheads were labeled as "idiots" or "the most disgusting of them all." He wrote his comments methodically, either directly on the newspapers or on pieces of paper. In this way, he had been leading his own political crusade for almost twenty years, up until his mental abilities and his memory started to falter.

No one had seen this material until 2007, when I opened the boxes that documented his political engagements and hatreds, almost everything that had occupied him for all those years, especially in the 1990s. He called it a "general cleaning up" after his return from a "period of exile." He had kept his mouth shut for more than forty years after being released from the prison camp in 1947 without truly being freed. Now he was striking back, and there were many people who had to pay. All his pent-up resentments flowed out in a frantic search for people he considered traitors. Writing comments on newspaper articles and drawing crosses on pictures of people he despised was his form of rebellion and his main way of communicating. But there was no one who could hear him, so he began to record the cassettes for me, talking about his life, the war, how screwed up the world was, and how terrible Norway's leaders were.

He had become a nationalist opponent of immigration by the end of the 1980s. In 1983, he retired after years working as a popular security guard at the Norwegian Academy of Music.[1] After that, he was left with only himself to think about, alone as he was after he and my mother parted ways. Eventually, he became overwhelmed by bitterness and anger about his fate and especially about the dangers he thought were threatening Norway. He turned to political activism but mostly without leaving his own living room. The thoughts and opinions that he had secretly hoarded inside him, perhaps even since before 1940, rose to the surface. They erupted in a new wave of fanaticism.

Things really took off in 1989, when he bought Peter Normann Waage's book about Islam and Europe, *When Cultures Collide* [*Når kulturer kolliderer*]. It helped to trigger his fear of Muslims, and he commented in the margins on page after page, expressing his shock and disappointment. When the Progress Party [Fremskrittspartiet] criticized asylum seekers and immigrants, it emboldened him. He had refrained from any political activities for years, but Carl Ivar Hagen, the party's leader, had unleashed something in him. Finally, a man who was willing to point out the real problems, someone who wanted to keep us safe from destruction! He joined the Progress Party in August 1989. "Carl Ivar was like a God to me," he explained. "It felt as though there was finally someone I could rely on again, someone I could follow."[2] Even though he thought Hagen was a politician worthy of admiration, the party did not go far enough on the issue of immigration, in his opinion. But he was riled up and ready to do his part to shift Norway's course and to stop the immigrants, the "foreigners," from taking over the country. His xenophobia was supported by what he witnessed on Torggata, the street where he lived in the center of Oslo. He was surrounded by what he disliked: immigrant groceries, kebab shops, and Asian restaurants. "The foreigners wander around in the streets here," he said, "speaking all sorts of different languages. I wish I could live somewhere else that was still centrally located." And yet Torggata was the perfect place for someone who hoped to have their views about what they thought was a frightening development confirmed. Even if he didn't like living "right in Oslo's most troubled area," this location had its advantages: "It's really an excellent observation post for my particular sort of research."[3]

Every day, my father would find new proof of how bad things were getting, especially in the newspapers. While the Progress Party continued to disappoint him by not taking a strong enough stance, he was still excited about Hagen and even noted that the party's leader had a moderating effect on him: "Without Hagen, many of us would probably have been incorrigible and out of line."[4] Another political party he supported was called Stop Immigration [Stopp innvandringen], which claimed that Oslo and Drammen would soon "be overtaken by foreigners." Such intentionally exaggerated and racist rhetoric made him even more zealous. For many years, he continued to support similar groups, both politically and economically (with thousands of kroner in donations), for example the Fatherland Party [Fedrelandspartiet] and the White Voters Alliance [Hvit Valgallianse]. He subscribed to the radical right-wing *Norsk Blad*, which argued that the Progress Party was not nationalist enough, and he also donated to *Fritt Forum*, a combative organ of nationalism. In addition, he subscribed and donated to the newspaper *Folk og Land*, which was published by a group of his former front soldier comrades.

The Institute for Norwegian Occupation History, which was founded and run by former members of the National Unification Party, wanted Petter to join their group, but he never attended their meetings. In one very important respect, he disagreed with them: it was simply not possible to deny that millions of Jewish people had been killed during World War II. When his old friend Ola Rishovd passed away in 1994, he got into a fierce debate about the issue with the former front soldier Arne Borgir, who was a Holocaust denier.

Eventually, my father made it known that he was a friend of the Jewish people and of Israel. He found it strange that the left could deplore "the way the Germans treated the Jews during the war" while also embracing the Palestinians who wanted to "banish the Jews from the so-called occupied territories." His defense of Israel was inextricably linked to his view of Muslims, who he saw as a threat to Israel's existence.

The apartment he lived in was like a prison cell. He felt confined and surrounded by foreigners, and in a sense, he was, since he lived in a part of Oslo with one of the highest number of immigrants. It was like fate had played a trick on him. In the early 1980s, he had lived in a small room in Tøyen, a central Oslo neighborhood, but it was so dreary that he applied for assistance from the city's housing agency. That was when the apartment in Torggata became available—he later wished he had never moved there.

Driven by fear, he kept up his incessant work of cutting and collecting newspaper articles. He used all his energy and worked without resting.

I was so obsessed and upset that there was almost no difference between day and night for me; I woke up in the middle of the night and felt ready to fight, and I would scribble down some notes to be "archived" the next day. . . . This was a time when I was completely absorbed in politics, elections, radio programs, TV, and discussions in the street, so there was hardly even time for meals or sleep.[5]

The things he wrote attest not only to his deep-seated fear but also his despair over not having anyone he could talk to. He felt isolated, and he was. In such a state, he saw threats everywhere and became paranoid: "Don't people realize that the foreigners, with their increasing participation in the workforce, will soon be able to create a great deal of trouble through an attack of some sort—the tram, the bus, the taxis, the cleaning services, hospitals, elderly care services?"

I too became a target of my father's harsh criticism: people on the left and especially the "Marxist-Leninists," a group I had belonged to when I was younger, were the absolute worst. To a certain extent, he could understand why I ended up so far out on the left, in opposition to society, considering my background and childhood. But he could not understand why I had taken it to such an extreme or accept it.

He was anxious about many things, including the risk of a break-in or other criminal activity. He had reason to be concerned, as the media kept reporting about burglaries and elderly people who were robbed in his area. His housing arrangement didn't make matters easier, as he lived in a neglected and deteriorating backyard apartment, which he left as little as possible. Feeling surrounded, almost occupied, he conflated the present with his wartime experiences: "Almost everything I do these days, what I think about and how I feel, is bound up with the desperate situation our country once again faces—just like in those terrible days in 1940 when the German airplanes thundered over us, and foreign soldiers flooded the country. Now airplanes full of foreigners are arriving, and we hardly even notice it."[6]

It is difficult to understand how it was possible for my father to make this comparison. Clearly, he was ignoring the fact that he was one of the people who "welcomed" the German planes. His way of avoiding responsibility and his interpretation of the events of 1940 confirms what German scholars have found in memory studies about World War II. According to Claudia Lenz, who has researched this topic in Norway, former Quisling supporters "interpret postwar history as a story of decline."[7]

My father thought that what he saw on Torggata was representative of the country as a whole and concluded that Norway itself would cease to exist: "I can imagine Norway a hundred or two hundred years from now, with around eight to ten million inhabitants and something like a hundred different languages, and five or six religions all fighting against each other. Constant riots and commotion in the streets—like a civil war! Whatever happened to being Norwegian?"[8] In his eyes, such a future could be avoided only if people supported the anti-immigration parties. If the majority of Norwegians didn't wake up, it would be a catastrophe. He was pessimistic, writing that "things have probably gotten too bad already—or is there still a chance to stop the Muslims from taking over Europe? What's frightening is that there is only one major Norwegian politician (Carl I. Hagen) who has the courage to speak the truth!"[9]

His despair over what his life had become only served to confirm his status as an outsider. As a young man, he had been a lonely soul, and so he was in old age. He was withdrawn and isolated from others, thinking that they wanted nothing to do with him. On that point, he was pretty much correct.

Even I had no idea that my father still held such extreme opinions, until I started to dig through the newspaper clippings. Of course, I had been avoiding him for a long time. But he still had other thoughts and feelings, even longings. He was more than just a tangle of rage and anger. There were times when he looked back on his life with warmth and fondness, including in the cassette recordings he made for me. One such recollection was from when I was three or four years old and we lived in a wooden house on Kirkeveien in Oslo, before it was torn down. I had misunderstood what someone in the neighborhood had said about my father, and I shouted up to him at the window where he stood, "Papa, you were never in the fire brigade, were you?" Fire brigade, he thought. What was Bjørn talking about? It took a few seconds before he realized what this strange question meant. As a little boy, I had been obsessed with firemen and the noisy red trucks that sped through the streets, and I had somehow gotten the idea that firemen started fires rather than putting them out. He then realized what had happened. To bully me, someone had brought up the fact that my father had been in the "front brigade" during the war, but I confused that with "fire brigade." Considering my understanding of what firemen did, I must have thought this was terrible. Who would want a father who had been in the fire brigade! "No, Bjørn, rest assured, I've never been in the fire brigade," my father replied. There was a certain kind of logic in the mistake: front brigade, fire brigade. And in a sense my father had been involved in starting fires. War itself is a fire that burns into your memory.

My father never forgot this little story, but he kept it to himself. Apparently, my naïve concern that he had been an arsonist or done something wrong made an impression on him. I can only vaguely remember what happened between us on that summer day in Oslo in the early 1950s, but it struck a chord. When I heard the story on the cassette, it changed the way I saw his life and how I felt about him. Maybe he had some redeeming features after all.

He also had a sense of humor. One day in 2004, he received a letter that he initially thought was a mistake. Norway's Resistance Museum was offering a commemorative silver medal for purchase, which was inscribed "Norway at War—Norway Liberated 1945"[10] The decoration depicted King Haakon's return from Great Britain on June 7, 1945. The offer was signed by the resistance hero Gunnar Sønsteby, who had been among the people my father pursued as a police officer during the war. Now Sønsteby, of all people, had sent this offer. On the day King Haakon returned, my father was imprisoned at Ilebu. It appears that Samlerhuset, the company that produced the collectible medal, assumed that a man in his age group would be part of the target market. The letter stated that the medal was "for people interested in Norwegian war history." My father saw the irony in the situation. On the envelope, stamped with the Resistance Museum's logo, he wrote, "Is this some kind of sick joke? Or has someone there finally realized what a valuable person I am?"

One year later, he moved away from Oslo, and the stress eased up.

PART III

CHAPTER 11

Black Dogs

It took me a long time. I had to think it through carefully, but I wanted to see the fields of grain and the plains full of sunflowers, to tread on the black soil that my father says is so fertile. I simply had to experience the landscape and the colors that my father saw when, as a young elite soldier, he was part of one of the most brutal military campaigns in history.

It was a journey into my own past, as my father's story had become mine as well. What took place in Ukraine left a mark on me, maybe even more than I dared to understand. Shouldn't I see it for myself? I wanted to follow in his tracks, to see the places where he had been, on foot or in a vehicle. In truth, I was only going to retrace a small part of the route he took, but still . . . I might in some way get to know more about what he had experienced. Would there be anything more to see, anything new to discover?

It was a July day in 2005, and only a few seats were empty on Tyrolean Airways flight DS 0381 from Vienna to Lviv. Some Americans were also on board, searching for their family's roots and hoping to learn more about their heritage. In the United States and Canada, there is a large and vocal group of descendants of Ukrainians who were forced into exile after the Soviet Union reconquered the country in 1944. There are also Jewish people with a Ukrainian background in the US, many of whom have attempted to trace their family histories. Following the Orange Revolution in 2004, a mere thirteen years after the fall of the Soviet Union and the reestablishment of Ukraine's independence, many people in the exile community felt hopeful about their country.

In Western Ukraine, left-leaning groups have traditionally been quite strong, and Lviv has always been a meeting place for travelers from countries such as Russia, Poland, and Germany. The name of the city is Lvov in Russian, Lwów in Polish, and Lemberg in German. It has been a target for conquerors of various nationalities, including Turks, Tatars, Poles, Germans, Austrians, and Russians. The Swedish warrior king Charles XII occupied the city in 1703 before suffering his greatest defeat six years later at Poltava, farther to the east in Ukraine. Capturing Lviv is not the same thing as conquering Ukraine, as the Germans too would learn.

Flying from Austria to Ukraine felt natural to me. My father had also departed from Austria with Regiment Nordland, which then marched through Poland and toward Lviv. He once scribbled on a letter I sent him, which I later found at his apartment, "Regiment Nordland advanced so quickly that it was impossible to follow their movements. Lviv and Ternopil were our destinations."

With no one else except my interpreter, I was about to embark on a journey through Western Ukraine. The route I had chosen was only 150 kilometers, from Lviv to Ternopil. It would have been too demanding to retrace my father's entire journey toward the Caucasus. But it was on this stretch of their route, between Lviv and Ternopil, that the German occupying forces and the Norwegian front soldiers first encountered the Ukrainian Jews. I had a bad feeling about what I might find. I knew that the Norwegians must have witnessed and taken part in atrocities. There was simply no other possibility.

~

Dawn was approaching. Hotel Sputnik, on the outskirts of Lviv, was built in the 1960s when quality was not a high priority, and little seems to have changed at the hotel since then. Its name comes from the first Soviet satellite that was sent into space in 1957, when Ukraine was part of the vast realm that was ruled from Moscow.

My first night in the hotel was disquieting: western European businessmen were targeted by beautiful women watched by tough-looking men who waited outside. The dogs outside were silent at night, but as soon as morning came, and the first streetcars started to pass by, they all started to bark, as though the high-pitched noise from the streetcar rails was the signal they had been waiting for. A guidebook advises, "All over Ukraine's larger cities, stray dogs move about in large packs and scavenge for food. . . . Remember that these are wild animals that have been known to attack individuals."[1] The text is clear as day, but I hadn't really imagined that there would be packs of wild dogs in the center of Lviv, a city that has been an important cultural center for over seven centuries. When I mentioned it to Ludmilla, the interpreter, she brushed it off: "Those dogs aren't a problem." No one seemed to care about the wild dogs. They had been there for so long.

But still unpleasant thoughts and associations crossed my mind. I thought of dogs searching for something to eat on a battlefield. I thought of the Norwegians who voluntarily fought here on the German side as dogs of war, trained ideologically by the officers in the Waffen-SS. My overall mission, to follow the trail of war in Western Ukraine, easily led me to thoughts about black dogs and black uniforms. I also thought of another dog: Laika, the stray who was picked up from a street in Moscow and placed on board Sputnik 2 and became one of the first animals in outer space. After a few hours, she died of stress and heat. Laika was tamed for her purpose, but it was too late to domesticate the stray dogs outside Hotel Sputnik.

With the gray morning light came rain. I stood in my hotel room on the seventh floor and looked out the window at the dogs as they restlessly ran in circles between the apartment buildings, which looked like the barracks of a defunct army. Later, Ludmilla showed me the center of Lviv whose architectural quality was much higher. There were stately, imposing buildings and many historical memorials, but there were also other signs of the past: on the remains of what had been a synagogue, someone had written racist phrases and anti-Jewish slurs. In one spot, "death to the Jews" was written. On a wall, someone had drawn a gallows with a Star of David hanging from the rope and a swastika above it. On the memorial plaque for what remained of the old synagogue, two swastikas had been drawn. Throughout the Jewish quarter, once a living and breathing part of the city, antisemitic epithets were scrawled on the walls.

In recent years, some Jewish people have moved back to Lviv from the places where they fled during the war. However, there is little interest in the fate of the Jews during World War II in today's Ukraine and even less interest in bringing to light the fact that Ukrainians participated in the killings. The country's dramatic war history hardly fits in with the self-image of the new Ukrainian state. Many people are afraid that the Ukrainian Jews who perished in the Holocaust will be forgotten.[2] Memorials and monuments to the Ukrainian nationalists are prioritized instead, and many of them helped the Germans in the hunt for Jews. Ludmilla said that there had been around seventy synagogues in the city before the war but that all except three were now gone or used for something else. Lviv is a city with a long Jewish history, but today's antisemites are doing their best to remove any trace of it.

Ludmilla comes from a Jewish family herself, and she watched with sadness and disdain as the authorities allowed the few remaining reminders of the city's Jewish history to fall apart. Only in recent years did she grow more conscious of her Jewish background, becoming active in a Jewish organization. She was not convinced that being a Jew in Lviv had gotten any better since Ukraine's independence as compared to the Soviet period. The country's nationalism had had many negative effects, she argued.

Ludmilla asked many questions, and I got the impression that she wanted to know more about what I was doing. Maybe she was worried that I would try too hard to understand the motivations of the Norwegian volunteers who enlisted on the German side.

"You need to put it into perspective," she said. "Do you want to punish your father, do you want to pass judgment, or are you doing this for your own sake? Does it really matter to you how many people he killed? He was here in Ukraine as a soldier—isn't that enough for you? How many Jews does he need to have killed for you to call it a crime?" Those were the kinds of questions she asked. Only later did I realize that she had understood from the start exactly what I was doing. She understood that I had no sympathy at all for the soldiers who invaded Ukraine; she just wanted to test me.

Ludmilla's family made it out in time. Her grandfather was a member of the Communist Party and a stationmaster in Klepariv, a suburb of Lviv, which would turn out to be crucial to their escape. Due to his membership in the party, the family was evacuated before the Germans arrived. Later, the remaining Jews in Lviv who had survived the depredations of the invading army were sent like cattle from the station where Ludmilla's grandfather worked to the extermination camps. Some of them ended up in Belzec, the camp north of Lviv, while others were sent farther west. In Janowska, a camp not far from the center of Lviv, 200,000 people were killed, most of them Jews.

What did the soldiers in the invading army do when they arrived, stuffed full of anti-Jewish propaganda? Did all of them hate the Jews? That was something I had been thinking about since I was twelve years old when I was reading about Operation Barbarossa and realized that my father had been there.

~

Lviv is gray and dirty, but there are lush green maple and hazel trees along the road out of the city to the east. In some places, it looks like a beautiful tree-lined avenue. The landscape rolls gently, with soft hills and knolls, grain fields, and tiny villages. Although the main road is paved, it is full of pot-holes and worn down on the shoulders.

Not many cars were to be seen as we drove east, mostly just old trucks carrying bricks or timber. Occasionally, we were passed by reckless drivers who didn't seem to care if there was a car coming in the opposite direction. Women in shawls stood along the roads selling vegetables, perhaps just like they did when my father was advancing on this road with his comrades in Regiment Nordland. Maybe at that point the road was made of gravel rather than asphalt.

I pictured him here, sitting on an army truck or walking along the road. Utility vehicles, armored personnel carriers, and maybe some motorcycles too must have been all around him. All of them pushing eastward in an endless torrent, hunting for the enemy. His regiment had stayed back for a while after the first wave of invading troops. They had received orders to strike down whatever resistance remained. Patrols went on detours, and if they found any enemy soldiers or "Jewish Bolsheviks," they probably made short work of them.

As we drove past a fertile field, I was reminded of something that had been promised to my father and his comrades when they first enlisted in the German army. After two years of service, they were supposed to receive "an existing farm with sixty to seventy-five acres of good farming land." If Germany had won the war and my father had settled down here, perhaps I might now be the owner of a farm in the German protectorate of Ukraine, thus realizing the goals of Hitler's Generalplan Ost. As the son of a Ger-manic colonial settler, I would have had servants, or even slaves, like in the old South in the United States. But it would have taken more than just

Germany winning the war for this plan to work. Many people like me would have had to identify as Germanic in our hearts and minds.

I was jolted back to the present day when we passed a horse-drawn carriage with two boys in it. One of them was playing with a mobile phone, as if to show that even people in Ukrainian villages were keeping up with progress.

~

A small river runs through the town of Zborov, which lies along the main road between Lviv and Ternopil.[3] This was the same route that my father followed eastward with Regiment Nordland, with short detours to the north and south.

The eighty-year-old Paltsan Pavlo work up early that morning, and he was ready to talk about his experiences from long ago to anyone who would listen. It was a warm day, and we strolled over a narrow wooden bridge where the river curves along a field. In Zborov, where 1,800 Jewish people lived when the war broke out, the year 1941 was dramatic and intense, as it was in many other towns and cities in Western Ukraine during the Germans' invasion. Paltsan lead us on the path and stopped to point out a memorial that had been raised on the field.

"Right down there is a very fertile area with a lot of good grass," he said. "That's where I would take the geese every day. It was my job to look after them."[4]

On July 3, 1941, the fourteen-year-old Paltsan was walking out to the river with his geese, using a cane to keep them under control as much as possible. As he approached the river, he noticed that something was about to happen a few hundred meters up the road. Soldiers with rifles were directing a large group of people down to a small field on the other side of the river. Some of the men were wearing long, dark coats and hats; their distinctive curls indicated that they were orthodox Jews. Many of the others looked like ordinary Ukrainians.[5] As the group came closer, Paltsan could see military vehicles and trucks behind them. He quickly hid behind some trees; the geese would have to manage on their own.

When the people got to the field, the first group of Jews were forced to take their clothes off. Some graves had already been dug out, and they were forced to line up next to them. It all happened very fast. They were shot one by one right then and there. Not much farther away, others stood waiting for their turn.

Paltsan snuck away and ran home to his parents to tell them about what he had seen down by the river. It turned out that others in town had also heard about the event; rumors traveled fast. Paltsan was not completely sure when I asked, but he thought that Ukrainians had helped the soldiers look for the local Jews. Two massacres took place there that day. Between 600 and 850 Jews were killed in a matter of hours, and their clothes were burned. Their houses were emptied out by the German soldiers who came later, and some neighbors also helped themselves to the Jewish people's property. The Jews who weren't killed that day were sent to a camp and killed later.

Paltsan never forgot what he had witnessed.

"I think about it often, and sometimes I go to the memorial with some of the other old people to pray."

"Are the remains of the people who were shot still buried here?"

My question lingers in the air for a while.

"No, I don't think so," Paltsan finally replies. Perhaps he was afraid of any follow-up questions or embarrassed that he couldn't give a clear answer?

We walked a bit closer to the field, but then Palstan stopped and said something to Ludmilla. He didn't want to come with us to the spot where it happened. We said our goodbyes and parted ways.

~

I walked down to the field. Almost without thinking, I kept an eye on the small hill, wondering if there was anything buried underneath. On the field where the Jews were shot, the upper layer of earth had been shoveled away. The field was going to be evened out, maybe even paved. Excavators had removed earth and stones from the site where a town marketplace was to be built along the idyllic riverfront. A memorial for the massacre of Jews was no longer suitable for the town of Zborov. The memorial had been built by the Geiger family, a Jewish family from the United States with roots in Zborov and Ukraine. The candleholder that had originally been part of the memorial had been stolen or destroyed. On the way to Zborov, we had stopped at a magnificent monument, in beautiful white stone, to the Ukrainian nationalists who fell in the war. The contrast between the broken Jewish memorial and the stone monument was striking. In Ukraine, some people are more worthy of remembrance than others.

Suddenly, I saw something white sticking out of the ground. Somewhat shocked, I carefully dug down with my foot to reveal more of the white object. Ludmilla saw what I was doing and walked over to me. It was definitely a bone. Could it be the remains of someone who died here? Or was it from an animal? The whole experience was unreal and frightening. Two men who had followed us from a distance noticed our reaction. They started to have an angry-sounding discussion. Maybe they didn't like the fact that someone was digging around in an area that the townspeople wanted to forget about. We felt threatened, and as we had already seen enough, we went back to the car and drove through the town before moving on.

Zborov consists mostly of simple wooden houses; it seemed like an unremarkable and poor town. Old cars cruised down roads without asphalt or gravel, leaving dust to hang in the air. Ducks, geese, and cows used the same roads, along with a dog or two. Women wearing large headscarves peeked at us from behind the picket fences where they stood in small garden plots. Some of the younger women looked a bit more modern. A church stood where a synagogue had once been. Jews no longer lived in the town.

Had my father really been here? While I was down by the river, I found it impossible to imagine. I preferred to believe that he had never been in Zborov. But if he had in fact been here, what did he do?

~

What I learned by the river in Zborov reminded me of the work that has been done in recent years by Patrick Desbois, a Catholic priest from Paris. In 2003, he traveled to Rava-Ruska in Ukraine to see for himself the place where his grandfather had been a prisoner of war. While there, he attempted to acquire more knowledge about what had happened to the city's Jews during the war. The mayor took Desbois to a grove in the woods where he was met by about a hundred elderly farmers who formed a circle and then told him what they knew and what they had witnessed. They pointed out several places where Jews had been buried after they were murdered by the foreign soldiers.[6]

His visit to Ruva-Ruska led Desbois to establish the organization Yahad–In Unum in 2004, along with other religious leaders such as Jean-Marie

Lustiger, whose Jewish mother died in Auschwitz.[7] The organization set up a professional team to investigate and map mass killing sites, which was led by Desbois and included French and Ukrainian members along with archeologists and pathologists. Since 2004, the team has filmed interviews with almost eight hundred Ukrainians who witnessed murders and massacres of Jews. Many of the witnesses say that they have never before spoken about what they know, and most of them have expressed a desire to tell someone about it before they die. The team has visited many villages in both Western and Eastern Ukraine. From the interviews, Desbois was able to get a clearer picture of how the killings and systematic executions were carried out. The objective was to kill everyone who was captured, although some people survived by hiding among the piles of corpses and were thus able to give their testimony.

According to Yahad–In Unum, 80 percent of the Jews who were killed in Western Ukraine were shot, meaning that most of them did not perish in the so-called labor camps. In many cases, the victims were forced to lie down on top of those who were already dead before being shot from above—the Germans called this "sardine packing." As of 2007, the organization has mapped five hundred execution sites and many mass graves. Not far from Lviv, fifteen mass graves have been found in the town of Busk alone, and Desbois believes that there must be at least 2,500 mass graves in Ukraine, many of which have no doubt already been plundered by grave robbers.[8] Many bullets, ammunition shells, and weapons have also been found, leaving no doubt that it was German military divisions who were behind the killings, even though some people in Ukraine still blame the Red Army and the Soviet Union.[9]

~

Who exactly was responsible for killing the Jews in Zborov? Was it the German army, the Waffen-SS, German police troops, or the *Einsatzgruppen*? Some evidence suggests that Regiment Nordland was nearby at the time, and so it is possible it could have been involved with the killings. According to a report from SS-Hauptsturmführer Böhmer, the regiment was two kilometers west of Zborov at around ten in the morning on July 3, 1943. They were marching eastward from Zloczov to Ternopil when they were joined by Böhmer's troops from the Second SS Panzer Division.[10] The report states that Regiment Nordland then moved farther north and took part in battles there.[11] It does not specify that the regiment went to Zborov, but it easily could have. Two kilometers is nothing for motorized infantry.

Documentary evidence shows that SS soldiers were responsible for the massacre in Zborov. On July 11, 1941, one of the Third Reich's most powerful men, Reinhard Heydrich, summarized the liquidations in the east in a report. Heydrich was the chief of the Reich Security Main Office in Berlin and one of the main architects of "the Final Solution to the Jewish Question." He was known as the "commissioner of the Jews."[12] His report states, "In Zborov, the Waffen-SS liquidated 600 Jews as a reprisal for a Russian attack."[13] The German historian Dieter Pohl claims that Division Wiking left a "bloody trail through Eastern Galicia, the troops kill[ing] prisoners of war and civilians." He writes that it was "most likely" soldiers from the Waffen-SS who killed the Jews in Zborov.[14] Everywhere on the route from Lviv to Ternopil, civilians and prisoners of war were killed by SS soldiers who were, by all accounts, from Division Wiking.

Paltsan Pavlo couldn't remember very many details about the soldiers and their uniforms since he was too far away. In his view, they were Germans, and it didn't matter to him if there were also volunteers from other countries among them. Considering the situation on the front near Zborov, it might have been the case that multiple units took part in the killings, not only the Waffen-SS.

In the small town of Zloczov, not far west of Zborov on the road to Lviv, reports were written that suggest that Division Wiking may have been involved in the mass killings there. On July 1, 1941, the Wehrmacht marched into the town, which two years earlier had had a population of 14,000, including 6,100 people of Jewish descent.[15] Strongly anti-Jewish Ukrainian nationalists helped the German soldiers find the Jews and took part in the massacres that started on July 3. One day later, reinforcements from the Waffen-SS came to the aid of the Ukrainian nationalists and the Wehrmacht. It is not known exactly which regiment it was, but Colonel Otto Korfes of the Wehrmacht's 295th Infantry Division later wrote in a report that the killings were carried out by "Ukrainians and the SS"—in this case, the SS would have meant Division Wiking.[16]

A letter from an anonymous Norwegian soldier who was in Ukraine at the same time as my father clearly expressed his reaction to what he saw:

"It is truly hellish here, and that is also why it is full of Jews. Most of them are gone now, but their stench lingers on, and we often find them in their hiding places. The world's plague, Jewry, will soon be gone from Europe. Never will I forget the ghetto in Lublin or the inexplicably mutilated corpses they left behind in Zloczov and Lemberg."[17] Were the Jews really the ones who left behind "mutilated corpses"?

Division Wiking left Lviv on July 1. A report states, "The head of the 4th corps reports that the division has been on the road between Lemberg and Zloczov since yesterday. Vehicles have been placed across the roads and blocked all traffic, . . . and they are refusing to let anyone through. In the meantime, some members of the division are out searching for Jews."[18] According to the German historian Bernd Boll, this meant that the soldiers shot "anyone who looked the least bit suspicious."[19] Division Wiking continued the bloodbath when it got to Zloczov.[20] The historian Saul Friedländer goes even further in his description of the events there: "In Zloczow the killers belonged first and foremost to the OUN [Organization of Ukrainian Nationalists] and to the Waffen SS 'Viking' Division, while *Sonderkommando 4b* of *Einsatzgruppe C* kept to the relatively passive role of encouraging the Ukrainians (the Waffen SS did not need any prodding)."[21] Boll writes that, in late June and early July 1941, thirty-five towns and villages in this area of Ukraine were sites of mass killings of Jews.[22]

That the Jews apparently put up very little resistance and did not make more of an attempt to escape from the atrocities may seem incomprehensible. Hans Friedrich, an SS soldier who was in Ukraine in the summer of 1941 and himself took part in the killings, described the Jews as "extremely shocked, utterly frightened and petrified, and you could do what you wanted with them. They had resigned themselves to their fate."[23] Helpless as they were, they became apathetic and ceased to resist. There was nothing they could do, and that is usually how people react when confronted with an enemy who is too powerful. Other testimonies have shown that when they did try to escape, it only hastened their death.

～

Less than forty kilometers east of Lviv, just north of the main route to Zborov, lies the small town of Hlyniany, surrounded by fields and wooded groves. The question running through my mind on the way there a few days after my visit to Zborov was whether my father had been there too. In 1939, there were 4,500 people living in Hlyniany, and 1,400 of them were of Jewish descent. The Jewish people of the town worked as artisans, bakers, doctors, and dentists. Many of them played an important role in the life of the community. There was a synagogue, a Jewish kindergarten, and a Jewish elementary school where the children could learn Hebrew.

Katerina Podolyak was ten years old when, in early July 1941, she looked out the window of her house and saw German soldiers shooting a group of the town's Jewish people. But there is another story she wants to tell me first about something she has never been able to forget.[24] Rumors about what the soldiers had done to the inhabitants of other towns and villages had reached Hlyniany. According to the rumors, they were even killing children, although not everyone believed it. When the townspeople heard that the foreign troops were approaching, a young Jewish woman came to Katerina's mother. She was carrying a newborn baby girl in her arms. Afraid of what might happen to her daughter, she pleaded and begged for Katerina's mother to take care of her.

At this point, Katerina paused, cleared her throat, and tightened her headscarf. She kicked aside some of the chickens who were strutting along the narrow street between the houses before continuing her story about what happened that day, which she thought must have been July 2, 1941.

"Please, you must take care of my baby," said the Jewish woman to Katerina's mother. "This is my only chance. I need to get away from here, and it's too dangerous to take her with me. I'll come back to get her when all of this is over!"

Katerina's mother was reluctant to help. A Jewish child! What would happen to her own children if the Germans found out that she was hiding such a thing? But she couldn't say no to the young woman who stood there, her eyes imploring. She accepted the tiny, crying baby and carried her inside, but she did not keep her at her own house. Right after the Jewish woman fled, Katerina's mother inquired around town to see if there was anyone who would take care of the baby. Finally, a woman in the neighborhood agreed. Katerina's mother never heard anything else about what happened to the child. The war and the invading forces made it hard enough for people to keep their own families alive and together.

In 1944, the Red Army liberated the inhabitants of Western Ukraine from the German occupation. The few Jews who had managed to escape could now return. One day, there was a knock at the Podolyak family's door. Young Katerina answered the door, and there stood the woman who had asked for their help more than three years earlier. Katerina's mother came to the door and heard the question she no doubt thought she never would: "Where is my child? Has everything gone well?"

Katerina's mother had to tell the truth: she had no idea what had happened to the child. She took the Jewish woman to the neighbor who had taken in the baby. The neighbor told them that the baby had been sent on from house to house. Everyone had feared the consequences of having a little Jewish baby at their home. And then the child was gone. This meant that she was dead, but who had killed her? Was it the soldiers? Or had one of the women who was supposed to take care of the baby taken her life to keep herself from harm? No answer. Katerina knows nothing about what happened—or does she not want to know?

Before I had a chance to ask any more questions, she turned away and said, "My mother never got over the fact that she didn't step up and take care of the baby." I sensed that it would be inappropriate to ask any more questions. There was not much left to say.

The story of the little girl who disappeared is one of many examples of an effect of the German invasion: a population divided against itself. When everyone's life is in danger, it doesn't take much for friends and neighbors to betray each other. At gunpoint, most people will save themselves and their families first. Informing on Jews at that time had few disadvantages, at least for some people.

We took a short break from the conversation before addressing what I really wanted to know. What exactly did Katerina see from the window of her house on that July day in 1941?

"With their heads hanging low, fifteen Jewish men from our town were led to the square right outside where my family lived," Katerina explained. "They had tried to escape but were arrested in one of the fields outside town. The soldiers kicked them and pushed them forward. Then they were shot right there. Other people had to bury them later."

Katerina could have closed her eyes or turned away, but she kept watching as the fifteen men were murdered. I asked her why they had been shot.

Did the soldiers think they were partisans, or was it merely because they were Jews? Katerina didn't know, but it was clear to her that the soldiers didn't want anyone to see what they were doing.

Later, more Jewish people in Hlyniany were killed. The few who managed to make it farther to the east never returned. In 1959, the town's synagogue, or what remained of it, collapsed. All traces of Jewish life and history in the town are gone, just like in Zborov and many other places. My father's great army tore communities apart forever.

$\sim$

I am back in Lviv at Hotel Sputnik; my short trip to Ukraine will soon be over. I have visited several small towns where Jews were massacred. I have spoken with many people, including a hundred-year-old woman and her daughter. In their town, soldiers set houses on fire and shot people in the streets. The elderly woman was so hard of hearing that her daughter had to shout my questions in her ear. She thought she remembered Norwegian soldiers in her town, or were they Dutch? In any case, they were blond. A photograph of one of them was taken when the daughter was two and a half. She was sure that his name was Erik, but the photograph was nowhere to be found.

Memory fails for many of the people who experienced the summer of 1941 in Ukraine. A long time has passed, and a lot of them are already gone. There are some questions we will never have answered.

One day remains before I return home. I call my father on the phone and get straight to the point.

"Do you remember the town of Zborov in Ukraine? All evidence suggests that you were there."

"Zborov," he says, repeating the name and tasting it in his mouth. I hear him take a breath. His voice is far away, but he is serious and focused. "No, I can't recall that name. You think I might have been there? You know, as ordinary soldiers, we didn't have maps. We hardly knew where we were or what the places were called."

"There are several sources, including a witness I have spoken with, that show that many Jews were killed there on July 3, 1941. Regiment Nordland might have been there."

"I see what you're getting at. You want to ask if I was involved in killing Jews. I can't remember ever taking part in killing civilians or knowingly and willingly killing Jews. But it is hard to tell how many bad things I actually did back then, since it was so long ago. I certainly have a guilty conscience about what I have done, but it was a war of life or death, and we were determined to stay the course."[25]

My father expresses himself slowly and clearly. He has been waiting for these questions.

CHAPTER 12

The Good, Difficult Discussion

His left foot has started to bother him. He avoided having it amputated during the campaign in Ukraine, but now it is hurting again. The war will not loosen its grip. His beard is whitish gray and lightens up his face. We started speaking to each other again when he was eighty-five, and now he is eighty-eight.[1]

We have both agreed to continue our conversations as much as we can, about the war in Ukraine and other issues that matter to us both. It isn't easy. He says that his mind is starting to "fizzle out" and that he has already forgotten so much. There must be a great deal he doesn't want to remember. One important question is how much of him there is in me.

"Does it feel like I've betrayed you by being critical of what you did in the war?" I ask him.

The question seems to surprise him, but I think he has expected it. He has occasionally brought up the fact that, when I was a teenager, I chose a political position as unlike his as possible. Perhaps he saw that as a betrayal on my part.

"Betrayed, you say? Well, I have tried to push that aside, I must admit. Of course, you grew up in somewhat reduced circumstances, so perhaps it isn't so strange that you were so far to the left politically. 'Betrayal' is a very strong word, and there's also a question of who betrayed whom. It has made me very sad that we have never really had a relationship with each other. I've often wished that we could have gotten along better and talked more about the war and my life. For me, it's completely idiotic that we weren't able to discuss this earlier."

"Do you see any similarities between your political choices and mine?"

It's a provocative question for both of us. My father joined the National Unification Party in the 1930s, and I joined the Worker's Communist Party (Arbeidernes Kommunistparti) a generation later. On paper, these two parties are polar opposites on the political spectrum. But perhaps such extremist political parties attract a personality type that we both represent. In my experience, we are both impatient, and we share an uncontrollable thirst for action and results. Willfulness and defiance are other traits I see in both of us.

"There's something to that comparison," he replies.

"At any rate, I've wondered what it is about us that led us to make such extreme decisions," I say.

"Ha! You can say that again. It's hard to know, don't you think? Is it even possible to answer that? I've looked to both sides, the right and the left. Haven't you also?"

"But you actually went to war on the side of the army that had invaded and occupied Norway, didn't you?"

"Yes, that's right. It sounds absurd today, and I sometimes ask myself if I truly believed in what I was doing. That decision cost me so much, not only a better relationship with you but so much else. That's why I'm glad that we can sit together like this now."

"You must have been quite firm in your belief if you enlisted in the war, right?"

"That's true."

"You were quite zealous as a Nazi, weren't you?"

"Yes, of course I was. When I think about it now, it just seems unreal. As time passed, and I started to see things more clearly, as you might say, it became totally incomprehensible to me that I was willing to sacrifice so much."

"How long did you define yourself as a Nazi? Your convictions didn't simply go away after the war was lost, did they?"

"It took some years. If I had immediately admitted to myself that I had made a mistake, it would have been a crushing defeat. But I did eventually."

"And yet you still defend your participation in the war against the Soviet Union?"

"Yes, my view of communism has not changed. I still think about it the same way that I did then—there was no other option. We had to be on Germany's side against Bolshevism. There is no doubt in my mind that Bolshevism was worse than what Hitler stood for."

"But you also say that what you witnessed in terms of the treatment of the Jews was traumatic for you, even all these years after the war, if I understand you correctly?"

"Yes, exactly."

There might be reasons that I cannot or don't want to understand that would explain why my father saw Nazism as a form of salvation. I have tried, to the extent possible, to put myself in his position. From the start, he was both a radical and a conservative but perhaps nationalist above all else. Most importantly, he was a poor working-class kid who went against the grain. But why did it have to be Germany? What did he think when he found out about the injustices committed against the Jews in Germany, especially after Kristallnacht in 1938?

"It's almost inconceivable to me that I didn't start to rethink things at that point. You always try to find an excuse for not doing this or that. The only thing I can say now is that I must not have been interested enough in the matter to stop and think about it. In retrospect, I've asked myself, what was I really doing then? That's my guilty conscience talking. If only I had taken it seriously enough, of course I would have reacted. Anything else would have been inconceivable. This is another issue you wanted to know about, right?"

"Yes."

"Why didn't you end it right there, you probably want to know. And that's exactly what I ask myself. It could be that I wasn't interested enough in politics, despite everything. And perhaps I simply did not prioritize what was happening to the Jews. I was influenced by the friends I had, and they were members of the National Unification Party who said that what the newspapers reported about the Jews in Germany was sheer propaganda."

～

It is a Sunday in late August. The sun is shining, and my father is sitting outside with his shirt off. His skin still has a summer tan. With his beard and his medium-length hair, he looks like a combination of his old idol

Knut Hamsun and an imam. He laughs when I say this, noting that he sees the irony. We have gradually started to approach the most sensitive topics.

"Why did you cry when Germany invaded Norway on April 9?" I ask him. "I would have thought that you would be happy about that."

"That's something I've thought about a lot. We needed to fight back against the Germans, and I was prepared to put up resistance. Now I'll become a soldier, I thought."

"But I thought that you sympathized with Germany's attack on Norway?"

"It wasn't so simple. The Germans were interested in gaining a foothold in Norway, especially along the coast. They were at war with Britain, of course, so eventually I saw that as an argument. Despite my disappointment, I accepted the situation."

"But it's still hard to understand why you enlisted to serve in the German army so quickly."

"I see why you're asking about it that way, and I admit that it's odd that I became pro-German again so fast. But what upset me most about the invasion of Norway went away once we got to know the Germans. Although I wasn't among those who spent the most time with the German soldiers in Raufoss, I did have friends who interacted with them every day. We got used to them; they were very disciplined, and of course they showed us their best side. They didn't act like vultures in that first phase."

~

Several months passed before we turned back to the war again. My father was waiting for the warmth of spring and summer to reenergize him. Why had it taken so long for us to discuss all this in the first place? Of course, I should have started to ask him about the war and his role in it many years earlier. Maybe then he would have been able to give more detailed and better answers. But it simply wasn't possible earlier—not for me.

"I've always wondered why you never wanted to talk about this," he says. "Others who were in the war with me say that their families, and especially their sons, have insisted on knowing more. 'Please tell us how it was!' they say. I think a lot of other fathers have opened up more and told their families more about their war experiences than I have."

"I wanted to keep it all far away from me. I didn't want to have a father who had been on the German side."

"As I've understood it, what you wanted most was to believe it never happened."

"Yes. At times, I've dreamed that it wasn't true that you were an eastern front soldier. But in the end, I realized that we had to talk about your past before it was too late for both of us. I want to know as much as possible about it. Your story is also my story, whether I want it or not."

"Having a shared history that we both understand has helped us have a more open and honest relationship. We have realized that this is how you think and this is how I think. And we have to come to terms with it."

"I still have a lot of trouble understanding how you could enlist."

"Do you think I have an easy time understanding that? How could I have wanted to go to war? That's a question I constantly ask myself. I don't think I can explain very well why I did it anymore. And you know, I have been troubled by a guilty conscience, both when the war was going on and afterward. It really hurts me to think that I have not always been honorable."

"What do you mean by that?"

"That I should have been on the other side, of course."

This statement hits me like a bolt of lightning. What in the world is he saying? Where did that idea come from? In all other contexts, he has been unwavering in his belief that supporting Germany was the only right thing to do. But his thoughts move in competing directions, and he also feels regret. It is just incredibly difficult for him to express it.

"Now you're confusing me. You believed in Hitler's Germany, and in that case, you couldn't have acted any differently. What you did only followed from your beliefs. Wasn't that the case?"

"Yes, of course that's right. I would have felt like a coward if I changed course. But it gradually dawned on me that Hitler wasn't the great man I had believed he was. Then I started to feel ashamed, but I choose to push those feelings away. It was too late anyway."

To feel ashamed? What did he mean by that, and when had he started to feel that way? Is this talk of shame just a rationalization after the fact? No answer. He has contradicted himself multiple times in our conversations. First, he says that he regrets enlisting in the war, and then he says the opposite. He is not used to answering questions about his past, which isn't so strange considering that he has mostly kept these experiences locked up in his own mind, talking about it only to himself. When he has spoken to others about the war, it has been with former comrades who allowed no room for any doubts. Then I show up with demanding questions and hold him accountable for something that happened long, long ago.

～

My father has not once set foot outside Norway since he returned from the war. He doesn't even have a passport. For a long time, I had planned for us to travel to Ukraine together, but then I abandoned that idea. It seems that he had seen enough of Ukraine.

"Have you ever thought about what would have happened if your side had won the war and the Soviet Union had lost?" I ask. "Do you think you might have stayed there? In Ukraine?"

"I would not have settled down and started a family there. I like Norway too much to have done that. I would have come home."

"You know that you could have been given a farm and land, right? Wasn't that tempting? I've seen for myself the possibilities there . . ."

"They have black soil there, which is incredibly fertile and free of stones. All you need to do is dig with a spade, like we did when we made trenches. I thought a lot about what it would be like to farm the land there. I come from a family of farmers, you know, so I could compare the land there to Toten—it was completely different. But I never considered the promise of land when I enlisted."

I change the subject.

"The Germans' goal was that the army would march over the Caucasus and capture the oil fields of Baku. Did you really believe that was possible?"

"I know it's hard to believe, but the plan was that we would ultimately get to bathe in the Caspian Sea. We were going to chase away the Russians, but of course we were the ones who were chased away in the end."

"The Caucasus remains a powder keg even today, with many powerful ethnic groups who want to govern themselves. What do you think would have happened if you and the Germans had shown up there as conquerors?"

"It would have been an endless war!"

～

Another autumn is approaching. With each visit to my father, there has been a question I kept putting off until later, out of cowardice and reluctance to put too much pressure on him. He is getting older fast. I need to ask him about everything, to get closer to the most painful and hardest issue for him to talk about: the murder of the Ukrainian Jews and the fact that many Norwegian Jews were also sent to their deaths. We have touched on this topic many times before; I have even read aloud to him what Norwegian war reporters wrote about how the Ukrainian Jews were treated. What role did he play in all this? In various forms, I have asked him the question "Were you directly involved in shooting Jews?" But it is like his memory vanishes into thin air as soon as we talk specifically about the killings. Nonetheless, he says that we must try to follow through with this conversation now that I have got him thinking more about the war.

"What were you taught about the Jews when you were at the recruit training school in Graz?"

"First, I should say that we didn't speak German very well at that point, so we didn't understand everything in the training we were given, especially not about what the Germans really wanted to teach us. For example, about what we were going to do and all that . . ."

"What kinds of orders did you receive about how to treat the Jews before the invasion of Ukraine?"

"I don't remember that. I'm not sure it came up as a topic. What we were told was that we shouldn't get involved with Russian or Ukrainian women."

"But you were not only going to war against the Soviet Union—your army was also going to wage war against the Jews in Ukraine, wasn't it?"

My question pierces right through him; I see that it shakes him up. It is the professional questioner in me, not his son, who is pestering him with questions like this. I don't enjoy playing that role and feel little desire to ask him the most penetrating questions. But I don't have a choice.

"I can't really remember that we were at war against the Jews," he replies. "I wonder if that's because I've pushed it aside, struck it from my memory, so to speak. I don't know if I've ever really absorbed it. But this is something that has bothered me my whole life. It was one thing to enlist in the war, but all this about the Jews is much worse, something else entirely. I still struggle with this, and I haven't ever been able to talk to anyone about what happened to the Jews either."

"But you must have been told before you invaded Ukraine that there was a large Jewish population there?"

"I only found out later that there were a lot of them in the areas where we went."

"Was that because you didn't see any of them or what?"

"It could be because they didn't stand out too much. It was never really clear to us who was who—Jews, Ukrainians, Russians."

"Are you sure about that? Or are you saying that because you don't *want* to remember clearly?"

"I do remember that the Ukrainians, to stay on our good side, would point the Jews out to us and say 'Jew! Jew!' They weren't so fond of the Jews either."

When I ask him what happened to the Jews who were pointed out in that way, he doesn't answer but says something about how he wasn't there. When I ask again, he repeats that the Ukrainian civilians tried to win "us" over by pointing out the Jews. I don't know whether this "us" means my father and his army unit or the Germans troops in general.

"There are written sources that show that Division Wiking, including Regiment Nordland, must have participated in the killings of the Jews, or at least been in the vicinity where such massacres took place, like in Zborov."

"That's something I wonder about. I'm being completely honest when I tell you that we never directly lined up Jews to shoot them. And we didn't hang them from ropes either, like what I've seen in pictures. We were not part of that. It must have been the Wehrmacht who did that."

After a moment of thought, he adds, "And yet we were supposed to have been the bloodiest ones."

~

My feeling of unease grows as I'm on the way to my father's place once again. There are still many uncomfortable questions left to ask, and I need to bring up other aspects of the military campaign in Ukraine. He has forgotten so much, but when we sit there across from each other, he is completely present—in the war. He seems to feel pressured, but I also notice that he thinks it's okay to talk together. It seems like he likes it too.

"How much brutality did you witness as the troops advanced into Ukraine?"

"If I remember correctly, it was like one big rush to get ahead at the beginning. After a while, it calmed down. We also became searchers who were given the unpleasant task of picking off the stragglers who remained in the trenches. That wasn't much fun. They thought they had saved themselves. They were shot."

When I yet again raise the issue of the large number of Jews who were killed, he says, "I have no doubt that many Jews were killed along the way as we advanced into Ukraine. That's how it was. But it was other troops who did that. They came after us and carried out cleanup actions in which Jews and other civilians were taken away. When I heard about it, a question went through the back of my mind; I asked myself why that was happening."

In a later conversation, he said that he must have slowly come to accept the atrocities being carried out against the Jews. As he explained, "I was fanatically pro-German and thought that everything the Germans did was right." When I try to take it further, saying that the atrocities he is talking about were happening all around him the whole time, we reach an impasse, and I move on to another subject.

"When did you first understand that the invasion of the Soviet Union was part of a larger plan that aimed to exterminate the Jews and other so-called subhumans?"

"That's something I still haven't really grasped," he says and looks away.

There aren't any suitable follow-up questions. Later, I bring up something he recorded on a cassette tape, when he compared himself to a Muslim warrior, even saying, "We must have been like the most fanatical fundamentalists who fight for Allah."

~

Shortly after my father returned from the eastern front, he signed up to serve in one of the organizations that watched over German-occupied Norway. The Germanic SS Norway played an active role in the deportation of the Jews in Norway. For a long time, I was afraid to find out that he had taken part in these activities. Fortunately, I did not find his name on the list of organization members who were involved. But he still has a guilty conscience about it.

"Have I managed to avoid thinking about this so much that I can't remember how involved I was? I can't even recall exactly what I was doing at that time. It's like there's a void there, something I didn't take with me. I don't really know how to explain it. It's like I didn't completely manage to follow along with the atrocities that were happening, like I couldn't take it in."

"But you knew about what was happening?"

"I probably thought that it wasn't really something worth talking about. It was more like it seemed natural that the Jews were being rounded up and sent away. What you all forget these days, which I would also like to forget, is that Norwegians weren't particularly fond of Jews in those days either."

He keeps returning to his mother and how she supported the Jewish people. Even as a very old man, he still hears her voice. He should have paid more attention to her religious love of the Jews, he says. Now it torments him that he didn't listen to her. And it pains him that he didn't take a stand, as he says, when he came home from the war and everything he had been through.

"The fate of the Jews is the hardest thing for me—that I didn't distance myself from the abuse and persecution of Jews. But it was like there was something in me that prevented me from speaking up."

"Well, you did continue to support the Quisling regime and the Germans, didn't you?"

"Are you asking me whether I remained firm in my support for all that even after the Jews were deported?"

"Yes."

"As I've said many times, this the most difficult part for me. I've been troubled by this my whole life. I later attempted to make things right somewhat by being a defender of Jews in any way possible. I've been a supporter of Israel for a long time."

～

In later conversations, we discuss my father's attitudes about immigrants. As previously mentioned, he welcomed the rhetoric of the Progress Party and Carl I. Hagen on this question. Eventually, he went even further in his opposition to immigration, supporting groups that were even more extreme than the Progress Party. This is hard for him to discuss now, as he knows quite well where I stand on the issue.

"There was a time when I did what I could to free myself from my earlier political opinions," he says. "But then the issue of immigrants came up, and it made me want to be engaged in politics again. That was when Hagen became like a god to me."

"In the 1990s, you would draw crosses on the foreheads of people in newspaper pictures who held opposing views about immigration. Why did you do that? Did you want them to die?"

"Those were the people I marked as charlatans who were only trying to exploit the situation Norway was in. They were Norwegians who thought more about their own careers than about our country, I thought."

"Where does this intense anger of yours come from, this hatred?" I ask him.

"That's probably hard to understand," he says. He doesn't add anything else.

~

My father left Oslo in 2005. Moving to the countryside saved him in many respects, and it also transformed him. He got away from all the changes that he found so threatening. He can breathe again, and we can approach each other with an openness we have never had before. Something else has happened that he never would have believed possible in the twenty years he lived on Torggata: his view of immigrants has moderated. He has even become friendly with a Muslim: his Pakistani doctor, Muhammed Iqbal, whom he brags about and praises to the skies. He sees Dr. Iqbal as the first doctor who is genuinely interested in his painful left leg. Dr. Iqbal has tried to ease the pain and wants to prevent the leg from amputation again, so many years after it was rescued the first time.

"You used to say that you didn't want immigrants as care providers if you ever moved to a nursing home," I say.

"I had to go to the doctor, and I heard that he was a good guy. So I thought, OK, I'll give it a shot. At my first visit, it turned out that he also spoke Norwegian well. We actually became what I would call friends."

"I never thought that you would end up being friendly with a Muslim."

"It's quite strange, yes, but I started to trust him and like him."

"Do you have a different view of immigrants now, compared to when you lived in the center of Oslo?"

"I think I have changed. I have seen that there are a lot of good people among them too. I used to think that they were mostly crooks who wanted to destroy us."

~

It is up for debate whether my father truly has changed or if his new view of immigrants is limited to his talented and charming doctor. His aggressive attitude toward politicians whom he sees as too pro-immigrant has long been a dominant feature of his thinking. Was moving away from Oslo all it took to change him? Or is he just agreeing with me to avoid further conflict? I try to take the conversation a bit further and tell him that I see a similarity between the harassment that Muslims are exposed to in Norway today and the way the Jews were treated in the 1930s.

"Maybe the Pakistani people in Norway are the Jews of our time, then?" I ask.

"Well, I understand your question, and I know the answer you're looking for. But it's too difficult for me to give you that answer. I'm just so far away from what I used to think back then."

~

I started this project and the conversations with my father because I wanted to understand his story and, in a sense, to overcome it. In addition to understanding him, I wanted to understand myself better. There haven't been answers to every question, but I did manage to get closer to him, and to myself, before it was too late. Yet what remains clear to me is that this story is the sum of everything that never should have happened. When you submit to a political project in the belief that it is the greatest and most important thing of all, you don't only lose yourself but you can also lose everything and everyone.

Epilogue

The Secret of the Little Wooden Box

The story of the beautiful wooden box from Ukraine and the story of my father belong together. There is no way to talk about one without bringing up the other. What I didn't know at first was that there was yet another story from the war hidden in the wooden box.

In January 1939, a young Jewish woman came to Norway. Ruth Maier had fled from Vienna, where Nazi racial theories reigned after Austria was annexed into Germany in 1938. Her sister, her mother, and her grandmother managed to make it to Great Britain; her father had passed away in 1933. The talented Ruth, who painted and wrote poetry, came to Oslo first, where she took the university admission exam at the Oslo Cathedral School after only a year. In the spring of 1940, she moved to Lillestrøm, where she lived in the home of a telegraph operator named Arne Strøm. Ruth's father had worked for the Austrian telegraph company, and Strøm was one of his contacts in Norway. In Lillestrøm, she met Agnes, who would later become my mother.

In the summer of 1940, after the invasion, Agnes was living with her older brother, Just, who had moved from Gjøvik to take a job in Lillestrøm. My mother met Ruth by chance on a street one day in June. Although Ruth was several years older, they formed a friendship, a friendship they both needed, as neither of them knew many other people their age in the area.

Lillestrøm had become an important and active industrial site; the Germans wanted to use it, for example, to expand the airport in Kjeller. People from many parts of Norway flowed into the town for work. When the Germans entered the town, it meant that what Ruth had escaped from and still feared had caught up with her. But she still felt herself to be free. She kept a diary in Norwegian and German, and she was happy that she had met someone she could talk to.

On July 17, 1940, Agnes turned sixteen, and Ruth baked a birthday cake for her. She used what little money she had left on the cake, as she wrote in her diary. But that was no problem, since Agnes had such beautiful and "Madonna-like" hair: "She lights up the whole room when she is here." My mother and Ruth took turns telling each other about their lives. Ruth recorded in her diary that Agnes did not want to get married. "I wouldn't dare; I want to be alone," she said.[1]

Ruth's diary contains many loving words about my mother, and she also wrote a beautiful poem she dedicated to her. When autumn came, my mother returned home to Gjøvik. But before she left, she received a small, square photograph of Ruth wearing a white blouse. On the back, Ruth had written in her small handwriting, "From Ruth to Agnes, August 1, 1940. Goodbye."

In 1941, Ruth moved back to Oslo, where she had become close friends with the poet Gunvor Hofmo. The two of them traveled around Norway together and worked small jobs where they could find them. In the autumn of 1942, Ruth did what she had always dreamed of doing: she became an art student—now she would become a real artist. But that was not to be. Nazism caught up with her, and in November 1942, she was arrested by Norwegian police. From the Oslo harbor, Ruth was sent to Poland on the German transport ship *Donau* and then to Auschwitz with several hundred other Jews. She died at the age of twenty-two.

In August 1942, my father returned from the eastern front. In his luggage was the little wooden box. One evening several months later, my parents met each other for the first time in Gjøvik, not long after Ruth Maier had been sent away to Auschwitz. Two years later, they were married at the city court in Oslo. My father signed the marriage license P. Westlie, but at the city court, he was registered as Vestli. Eventually, the name Vestli would disappear from the official documents. For a short time, they lived together in a room in Raufoss before moving to Oslo. Thus, my mother dared to do what she had told Ruth she didn't want to: she got married. And not just to anyone—her husband was a hardened Nazi. By all accounts, my mother knew at this point that Ruth had been deported from the country. But she had made a pivotal choice; she had chosen my father, despite the fact that no one in her family would ever accept it. Her brother was a communist who was active in the resistance. When she took the train from Gjøvik to Oslo to join my father, her mother ran after the train in total despair. She even broke a bone trying to stop the train, but it was no use.

Only much later, sixty years after Ruth Maier had given the photograph to my mother as her final farewell, did I realize how this was all connected. I had seen the picture of Ruth before but without realizing what it meant. I knew that my mother had once told me about how she had a Jewish friend. "She was gassed in a camp," she said. But I never had a chance to follow up on it before my mother lost her memory. When she died, I inherited the wooden box, but I didn't think about it too much and put it aside. When I finally opened it, I understood that the story of the wooden box had long been waiting there for me. My mother had placed two pictures inside it: the one of Ruth and the one of my father from the war years. In doing so, she had brought together several different histories and fates in that carved work of art that my father plundered in a war he never should have been part of.

When I traveled to Ukraine, I took the wooden box with me. I wanted to find out more about it. How had my father gotten his hands on it? Was it a war prize? I felt complicit in something I couldn't fully explain; I forgot about it in my luggage and then worried about what the customs officers might think if they found out that I had that sort of carved wooden box with me.

The historical museum in Lviv is housed is a large brick building, and some of Ukraine's foremost experts in artisanal handicrafts work there. The head of the museum's applied art collections, S. Bohdanov, inspected the wooden box for two days. The museum has several others of the same type. He explained that the box is made of linden wood and that it was created at some point in the 1920s in Western Ukraine. The hand-carved ornamentation is characteristic of that era, and the design is typical of traditional handicrafts made by the Hutsuls, an ethnic group whose folk art is distinct from other Ukrainian art. The Hutsuls have lived in isolation for centuries in the Carpathian Mountains along the border between Ukraine and Romania, southwest of Lviv. They are especially known for their wood carving, and their handmade products are also popular in other parts of

Ukraine. An unknown Hutsul artisan had made the carved box long before Operation Barbarossa would change its path through history.

I brought the wooden box with me to the town of Hlyniany when I met with Katerina Podolyak to talk to her about what she had seen during the war. When I asked her if she had ever seen other objects like it, it turned out that she had.

"There aren't many of those left," she said.

"What are they used for?" I asked.

"In the past, we would use wooden boxes like that to hold jewelry and money, and the Jewish people in town did so as well. But how could that have ended up in Norway?"

"My father took it when he was in this area during the war. But I'm not sure he was right here exactly," I said.

She reflected on it for a bit, then looked at me and said quietly, "I don't think anyone would have voluntarily given him such a finely made wooden box."

Then what had really happened to allow my father to take this war prize?

∼

When I returned home from Ukraine, the wooden box was again hidden in my luggage. Now it was my turn to bring it to Norway. When I showed it to my father during one of our conversations, he looked surprised. He lifted the box up, held it in his hands, and touched the patterns in the carved wood.

"What happened?" I asked.

He couldn't answer. Or did he not remember?

"It must have come from one of the farmers," he said. "But everything was chaos and ruins back then."

∼

In his novel *Call It Anger* [*Kall det vrede*], Per Malde depicts a son's relationship with his father, who was a member of the National Unification Party and still sticks to Nazism many years after the war. The son, Erik, searches for a way to justify his own life and his connection to his father. He asks himself, "What have I been looking for my whole life, if not a sense of decency?" With that in mind, he eventually travels home to his father for a reckoning. He nearly loses control, tearing Hitler's *Mein Kampf* and Knut Hamsun's collected works off the bookshelf and destroying the furniture. After this reckoning, he concludes that "all accounts are paid and settled" and that the relationship between him and his father has been emptied of emotion.

When I read the novel, I became morally indignant and thought that people don't do such things. But what have I done? Have my actions been any more "decent"? I snuck away and froze my father out. He became even more bitter and entrenched.

Most people with a traumatic history like my father have locked the door and thrown away the key, far away in the woods. He kept his key close, left it in the door—and in the end, he also left the door ajar.

But I only showed up when it was convenient for me.

Notes

Translator's Introduction

1. Stratigakos, *Hitler's Northern Utopia*, 14–15.

2. Martin R. Gutmann notes that "estimates of the numbers of German volunteers are hard to establish with certainty and vary from 60,000 to 130,000" (*Building a Nazi Europe*, 2).

3. Sørlie, *Solkors eller hakekors*, 7. Grimnes likewise estimates 4,500 to 5,000 (*Norge under andre verdenskrig*, 147).

4. Sørlie, *Solkors eller hakekors*, 8.

5. Grimnes, *Norge under andre verdenskrig*, 148.

6. Grimnes, *Norge under andre verdenskrig*, 155.

7. Grimnes, *Norge under andre verdenskrig*, 171.

8. See Fure, "Norsk okkupasjonshistorie." See also Grimnes, *Norge under andre verdenskrig*, 12.

9. Examples of recent book-length treatments of the topic include Sæther, *"En av oss,"* and Sørlie, *Solkors eller hakekors*.

Chapter 1. The Attack

1. Petter Westlie, cassette recording. The cassettes that Petter Westlie recorded and later gave to the author were numbered. They are sometimes but not always dated. When a source is not provided for a quotation from Petter Westlie, it is from one of these cassettes.

2. Victor Mogens was rightly fired as a commentator on the Norwegian public radio station for being too politically one sided. When he was forced to leave, Mogens received strong support from, among others, the newspaper *Aftenposten*. He was himself the author of the January 1937 brochure *Marxism Conquers Radio Broadcasting—Why I Am Leaving*. See Dahl, *Hallo—Hallo!*, 274–75.

3. This is now 20 Knut Hamsuns vei.

4. Heljar Westlie has been helpful in uncovering information about the West-lie family's property and relationships.

5. The facts about the industrial development of Raufoss are taken mainly from Wang, *RA i skuddlinja*, published for the centenary of Raufoss Ammunition Factory in 1996.

6. Kolloen, *Hamsun*, 73–76.

7. It was not only his literary works but also other sides of Hamsun that Petter would come to appreciate. Hamsun was highly critical of British people and culture but much more approving of German culture. Both Hamsun's outlook on life and his political views would greatly influence Petter.

8. The Raufoss Ammunition Factory changed its name to Raufoss AS in 1989.

9. Løvlie, "Norske våpen i tyske hender."

10. The Nicoline attic was named after a former female worker at Raufoss Cartridge Factory. She had lived for many years in the attic of the ammunition workers' building.

11. Telephone interview with Aud Blegen Svindland, August 30, 2007.

12. Dahl, Hagtvet, and Hjeltnes, *Den norske nasjonalsosialismen*, 130–35.

13. Myklebust and Hagtvet, "Regional Contrasts in the Membership Base of the Nasjonal Samling," 630.

14. Holmen, *Kaare*, 77.

15. Hegtun, *Rundt fabrikken*, 61.

16. Telephone interview with Aud Blegen Svindland, August 8, 2007. Svindland's brother enlisted as a volunteer soldier for the Germans.

17. The discussion of Eugen Rygel is based on newspaper clippings and other documents collected by the cultural department of Vestre Toten in connection with an exhibition of Rygel's artworks in 1999. Sverre and Esther Aaslund of Raufoss also contributed information. Rygel was convicted of and received a sentence for treason after the war.

Chapter 2. The Transformation

1. The Workers Federation of Sports was a national athletic association founded in 1924 as a league for the labor movement.

2. Hansen, "NS på Gjøvik 1933–1940," 17–22.

3. Pryser, *Klassen og nasjonen*, 184.

4. Trygve Lie had been appointed minister of state one year earlier. He quickly distinguished himself as a "law and order" politician, and in a debate in the Storting in 1936, he said that "it is the task of the state to keep the peace in society" as well as the task of the young workers. See Amundsen, *Trygve Lie*, 98.

5. Pryser, *Klassen og nasjonen*, 186–87.

6. Hansen, "NS på Gjøvik 1933–1940," 20.

7. One month before the winter Olympics in Garmisch-Partenkirchen, Sonja Henie had danced pirouettes on the ice in Munich, which greatly entertained Hitler. A photograph from the event shows Hitler greeting her after her performance. He can hardly lean in close enough to the blond Nordic Henie, the "häseken" (little rabbit) from the far north. Behind Hitler sits the propaganda minister Joseph Goebbels and the head of the Luftwaffe, Herman Göring. See Stenseth, *Sonja*, 126.

8. Whether or not the Nazi salute was given during the Olympics became a political litmus test for Hitler's regime. Athletes from all countries were therefore encouraged to salute the führer during the opening ceremony. The Norwegians were among those who did not obey the request—which made Hitler furious—even though the German envoy in Norway had in fact promised the Germans that the Norwegian athletes would comply. See Norges Olympiske Museum, "Garmisch-Partenkirchen," https://ol.museum.no/om-olympiske-leker/vinterleker/garmisch-partenkirchen-1936.

9. Schaap, *Triumph*, 193–95.

10. "Norske fotballgutter gjorde Hitler rasende."

11. Interview with Tore Pryser, Oppland University College, March 2, 2007.

12. The National Socialist Worker's Party was banned in 1940 after Norway was occupied by Germany and the National Unification Party became the only legal political party.

13. Fure and Jensen, *Mellomkrigstid 1920–1940*, 239.

14. Hitler was furious at the Nobel Committee and claimed that the selection represented a form of interference in German affairs. Many conservatives in Norway agreed, including Knut Hamsun. *Aftenposten* claimed that it was a "war prize," not a peace prize. On November 26, 1936, the newspaper published a lead article under the title "Mistake" in which it stated that "it would be highly regrettable if Germany understood the award as a protest against its form of government (Nazism)." Carl von Ossietzky died in a concentration camp in 1938.

15. *Oppland Arbeiderblad*, November 12, 1938

16. *Oppland Arbeiderblad*, November 14, 1938.

17. Mendelsohn, *Jødenes historie i Norge gjennom 300 år 1940*, 2:642.

18. Hem and Børdahl, "En nød som ord ikke kan beskrive."

19. Wang, *RA i skuddlinja*, 141.

20. Sivesind, *Motstandskampen på Raufoss 1940–45*, 27.

21. The Administrative Council was established by the Supreme Court and was operative in the period between April 15 and September 25, 1940. The occupying

Germans wanted to make the Administrative Council into a kind of countergovernment so as to legitimate the occupying regime, but Norwegian negotiators managed to limit its scope to civil administration. Johan Nygaardsvold's government in exile never accepted the Administrative Council as anything other than an emergency agency.

22. Ugelvik Larsen, "The Social Foundation of Norwegian Fascism," 606.

23. Holmen and Wang, *Vår kamp for rettferd og framgang*, 124.

24. Wang, *RA i skuddlinja*, 143.

25. Wang, *RA i skuddlinja*, 149.

26. Holmen and Wang, *Vår kamp for rettferd og framgang*, 123.

27. Holmen and Wang, *Vår kamp for rettferd og framgang*, 127.

28. Holmen, "Raufoss og andre verdenskrig," 155.

29. Conversation with Petter Westlie, April 15, 2006.

Chapter 3. The Path to the SS

1. Enlistment form for Regiment Nordland volunteers, 1941.

2. *Aftenposten*, January 15, 1941.

3. Sverresson Sjåstad, "Nordmenn i tysk krigsinnsats," 115. Sverresson Sjåstad shows that it is a myth that the Norwegian front volunteers were all young, although there were some very young people among them, including three who were only fifteen years old.

4. The information about Reidar Seeberg is derived in part from the obituary "Falt for sitt land," *Fritt Folk*, May 31, 1943.

5. "Vidkun Quisling: Opprop til 'nasjonalbevisste nordmenn' om å tre inn i 'Regiment Nordland,'" NRK, January 12, 1941, Nasjonalbiblioteket, Oslo, https://urn.nb.no/URN:NBN:no-nb_dra_1994–12052P; Quisling, *Quisling har sagt*, 59.

6. Before Quisling's call for Norwegians to volunteer for German military service, some very eager young Nazis had already tried to do so, but they had been told that the Germans could win the war without anyone's help. Some people also went to the Italian legation in Oslo to see if they could take part as volunteers in the Alpini, the Italian mountain infantry. They were accepted, but when the call from Quisling came, they chose to join Regiment Nordland instead (Jens Lund Berentzen to Bjørn Østring, January 16, 1992, in the author's possession).

7. Sørlie, Kott, and Emberland, "I krig for Hitler," 56.

8. *Aftenposten*, January 14, 1941.

9. On September 24, 1940, Reichskommissar Josef Terboven appointed many ministers of state who were each to control one specialized department; most of them were National Unification Party members, and Vidkun Quisling was given the role of political chief of government.

10. *Aftenposten*, January 16, 1941.

11. Sverresson Sjåstad, "Nordmenn i tysk krigsinnsats," 119.

12. Skjønsfjell, "Frontkjempere fra Troms," 72.

13. Petter's brother, Rolf Westlie, stated in conversation with the author on January 19, 2007, that it must have been a thirst for adventure or a sort of "youthful insanity" that led Petter to enlist.

14. "Mønstring av de første norske frivillige til 'SS-Regiment Nordland,'" NRK, January 30, 1941, Nasjonalbiblioteket, Oslo, https://urn.nb.no/URN:NBN:no-nb_dra_1994-12058P.

15. *Aftenposten*, January 31, 1941.

16. "Mønstring av de første norske frivillige til 'SS-Regiment Nordland.'"

17. Sverresson Sjåstad, "Nordmenn i tysk krigsinnsats," 48. It wasn't until Germany broke the nonaggression pact with the Soviet Union on June 22, 1941, that it became easier to recruit more Norwegians.

18. *Fritt Folk*, February 6, 1941.

19. *Aftenposten*, February 6, 1941.

20. *Fritt Folk*, February 6, 1941.

Chapter 4. The Soldier Factory

1. Per Pedersen, "På Wikingtokt," *Munin*, January 1945. "På Wikingtokt," which translates as "on a viking raid," was published as a series of articles in the Nasjonal Samling's illustrated magazine *Munin*. A nearly identical version of the series was also published in *Germaneren*, the journal of the Germanic SS Norway, in 1944, under the title "From Lublin to the Caucasus" ["Fra Lublin til Kaukasus"].

2. Petter Westlie to Rolf Westlie, February 18, 1941.

3. Pedersen, "På Wikingtokt," *Munin*, January 1945.

4. This reproduction of the daily schedule is based on a speech given at a veteran festival for former SS-Wiking soldiers on February 16, 1991.

5. Petter Westlie to Rolf Westlie, May 11, 1941.

6. *Oppbrudd*, 18–19.

7. *Oppbrudd*, 24.

8. Ulateig and Brenden, *Nordmenn på Østfronten*, 17.

9. Förster, "Die weltanschauliche Erziehung von SS, Polizei und Waffen-SS im Rahmen der 'Endlösung,'" 98–99.

10. Quisling, *Kampen mellom arier og jødemakt*.

11. Fjørtoft, *Veien til Østfronten*, 169. In German, the oath is "Ich schwöre Dir, Adolf Hitler, als Führer und Kanzler des Reiches, Treue und Tapferkeit. Ich gelobe Dir und den von Dir bestimmten Vorgesetzen Gehorsam bis in den Tod, so wahr mir Gott hilfe."

12. In the sentence for treason that Petter received after the war, it was claimed that he did not take any oath, because he was sick. Petter himself emphasized that this was a "lie." Everyone who wanted to go to war had to take the oath.

13. In *European Volunteers*, the historian Peter Strassner writes, "The Norwegian and Danes thought that their military training was more difficult than their German comrades. . . . The Danes were more robust and not as sensitive as the Norwegians. . . . The Norwegians worked harder and were more serious and thoughtful. They were quiet and had a more youthful and unworried nature, but when they first decided about something, they kept to it. In their military activities, however, they took on an intense focus that sometimes led them to be careless about their own safety" (9–10).

14. The British author and filmmaker Laurence Rees claims in *The Nazis* (167) that Hitler invaded Greece with his own soldiers because he did not have confidence in the Italian Fascist leader Benito Mussolini, who was in fact the one who should have been responsible for the occupation of Greece.

15. *Morgenbladet*, May 15, 1941. In addition, minister of state Jonas Lie's joyful message from the front was given special placement in *Morgenbladet*. An article with the title "Twenty-Five Thousand Jews in France Placed in Concentration Camps" was placed directly above the interview with Lie. The French Vichy Regime, which collaborated with the occupying German forces, had put the Jews to work on "reconstruction work." It is not known how Lie reacted to the layout of the articles.

16. Lie, *Over Balkans syv blåner*, 18–19.

17. Sverresson Sjåstad, "Nordmenn i tysk krigsinnsats," 78.

18. Pedersen, "På Wikingtokt," *Munin*, February 1945.

19. Pedersen, "På Wikingtokt," *Munin*, March 1945.

20. *Fritt Folk*, August 17, 1941. Later, Osvald Olsen was recruited to the division's propaganda unit as a war correspondent.

21. Braithwaite, *Moskva 1941*, 76.

22. Murphy, *What Stalin Knew*, xvi.

Chapter 5. The Storm

1. Subtelny, "The Soviet Occupation of Western Ukraine," 8–10.

2. *Aftenposten*, June 24, 1941.

3. Kosyk, *The Third Reich and Ukraine*, 150.

4. Speer, *Erindringer*, 158.

5. Fest, *Hitler*, 551.

6. Petter was in the first company and first battalion of Regiment Nordland. Between 4,500 and 5,000 Norwegians fought on the eastern front during the war.

An estimated 781 of them were killed on the battlefield or died while imprisoned. Fifty-five of them fell during the first year of the campaign. See Sverresson Sjåstad, "Nordmenn i tysk krigsinnsats," 78–81.

7. Petter Westlie, undated note, probably from 1995. There were also young men in Raufoss who wanted to enlist to fight the war on the other side—against Germany. Two months after Petter and his two comrades left Raufoss, Odd Andersen and Willy Myhre decided to join the Norwegian armed forces in Great Britain. They got into contact with the resistance movement in Oslo, which helped them across the border into Sweden. From Sweden, Andersen and Myhre went to Moscow to continue the journey from there. In the beginning of June, they were in Ukraine. They crossed the Black Sea on June 20, only one day before Germany attacked Ukraine, but they were able to make it all the way to Great Britain, where they enlisted for service in the Norwegian air force. See Sivesind, *Motstandskampen på Raufoss 1940–1945*, 29.

8. McCarthy and Syron, *Panzerkrieg*, 98.

9. Johansen, *Frontkjemper*, 36.

10. Norwegian News Agency report reprinted in *Fritt Folk*, July 19, 1941. The report is dated June 26, 1941. Along with a Danish colleague, Hartmann went to the front before Division Wiking arrived.

11. Lviv is called Lvov in Russian, Lwów in Polish, and Lemberg in German. In 1939, 160,000 Jews lived in Lviv, and 40,000 Jewish refugees from Poland came to the city in 1940. Within a year, half of them were dead. In July 1944, there were only eight hundred Jews remaining in Lviv. See Simon, Stratenwerth, and Hinrichs, *Lemberg*, 75.

12. *Hirdmannen*, August 16, 1941.

13. *Germaneren*, no. 11 (1942).

14. Quisling, statement to the Norwegian Supreme Court, November 11, 1945, in Kolsrud, "Kollaborasjon og imperialisme," 241.

15. *Morgenbladet*, June 24, 1941.

16. Rees, *Auschwitz*, 44.

17. Kosyk, *The Third Reich and Ukraine*, 138.

18. *Aftenposten*, August 5, 1941.

19. Quoted in *Fritt Folk*, July 19, 1941.

20. Some of the main officers who served on the eastern front did not agree with Hitler's strategy regarding the continued military advance into the Soviet Union. On August 17, 1941, the commander in chief of the German army, Walther von Brauchitsch, wrote a memo to Hitler that urged a faster advance toward Moscow. He wanted to take advantage of the good weather. Four days later, Hitler answered gruffly that conquering Moscow was not the most important goal of the operation

in the east. First and foremost, it was to capture the industrial and mining districts in the Donbas and cut off the Russians' oil supply from the Caucasus. The capital of Ukraine, Kiev, would be encircled, and the march east toward Baku over the Caucasus Mountains would continue with undiminished power. See, for example, Rees, *The Nazis*.

21. Petter Westlie, undated note.

22. Grossman, *A Writer at War*, 40.

23. *Hirdmannen*, August 16, 1941.

24. *Samhold/Velgeren*, September 2, 1941.

25. Petter Westlie to Rolf Westlie, September 9, 1941.

26. Ola Rishovd to Petter Westlie, December 19, 1993.

27. Petter Westlie to Rolf Westlie, September 9, 1941.

28. *Hirdmannen*, August 16, 1941.

Chapter 6. Limitless Brutality

1. Rolf Hobson, "Germaniseringspolitikken i Øst-Europa og Generalplan Ost," HL-Senteret, October 6, 2011, last modified April 29, 2020, https://www .hlsenteret.no/kunnskapsbasen/folkemord/folkemord-under-nazismen/holocaust/ operasjon-barbarossa-og-generalplan-ost/generalplan%20°g%20germanisering%2 outdypende.

2. Ever since the seventeenth century, any number of German poets, artists, and intellectuals had fantasized about Germany conquering colonies. This vision later developed into a colonialist current that was also clearly racist. See Zantrop, *Colonial Fantasies*.

3. One of the movement's goals was to gather together all German-speaking people politically. It was organized in 1894, when professor and member of parliament Ernst Hasse founded the Alldeutscher Verband. His intention was to raise national consciousness, especially among the Germans outside the borders of the German empire. The pan-Germanic ideology was strongly anti-Slavic and anti-Jewish ("Pangermanisme," Store norske leksikon, https://snl.no/pangermanisme).

4. Lower, *Nazi Empire-Building and the Holocaust in Ukraine*, 20–22.

5. Kosyk, *The Third Reich and Ukraine*, 78–80.

6. Hitler, *Mein Kampf*, 961.

7. Rees, *Auschwitz*, 38.

8. Front soldier songbook, published by the Front Soldier Office and National Propaganda Leadership, 1943.

9. Wibe, "Mennesker og jøder." Wibe later died on the eastern front.

10. Wette, *The Wehrmacht*, 93–94.

11. Matthäus, "Controlled Escalation."

12. Megargee, *War of Annihilation*, 67.

13. Wette, *The Wehrmacht*, 96.

14. Rees, *The Nazis*, 213.

15. Wette, *The Wehrmacht*, 128.

16. Nazi policies regarding Jews in Europe only took final shape six months after the start of Operation Barbarossa. This happened on January 20, 1942, at the Wannsee conference outside Berlin. Under the leadership of Reinhard Heydrich, chief of the Reich Security Main Office, fifteen central figures from the party and the regime planned how the "Jewish problem" would be solved. It was after this conference that the killing of Jews became an industrial project with death camps and gas chambers.

17. Landau, "Once Again I've Got to Play General to the Jews," 89.

18. Heer, "Hitler war's," 294.

19. Longerich, *Dette viste vi ikke noe om*, 176.

20. Magocsi, *A History of Ukraine*, 631.

21. The Soviet Union's annexation of Western Ukraine in 1939 strengthened Ukrainian nationalism and resistance. Pro-German and antisemitic groups in Ukraine actively supported the German invasion and cooperated with the occupying Germans in the hunt for Jews and communists. Even before the invasion, Ukrainian nationalists had cooperated with Germany, resulting in the formation of two army units—Nachtigall and Roland—that fought on the German side. The great famine at the beginning of the 1930s, during which millions of Ukrainians starved to death in the Soviet part of Ukraine, was said by many to have been caused by Soviet policies. See Subtelny, *Ukraine*, 312–15. The Ukrainian nationalists believed they would get their own state through an alliance with Germany, which had promised to dissolve the collectivized farms and give Ukrainians freedom of religion. In many towns and cities, therefore, the Germans were met with jubilation and flowers. The Germans systematically exploited these anticommunist and antisemitic sentiments. They distributed flyers in Ukrainian that promised to liberate the Ukrainians from "Jewish Bolshevism." See Lower, *Nazi Empire-Building and the Holocaust in Ukraine*, 37. It didn't take long, however, for it to become clear that the Germans would deny the Ukrainians' demands for freedom.

22. *Vestfold Presse*, August 10, 1942.

23. Neumann, *Dødens drabanter*, 125. *Dødens drabanter* was published in English as *The Black March*.

24. Neumann, *Dødens drabanter*, 140–41. On January 16, 1960, the newspaper *Folk og Land*, which was run by former NS members, harshly criticized Neumann's book and claimed that it must have been fabricated.

25. *Fritt Folk*, August 8, 1943.

26. "General Record of the Government Code and Cypher School and Government Communications Headquarters," HW 1/62, National Archives, Kew, Great Britain.

27. A message that was decoded on August 24, 1941, stated that the First SS Brigade "has taken 29 prisoners and shot 65 Bolshevik Jews," that "an Einsatzgruppe has shot 12 bandits and partisans, as well as 70 Jews," and that "Battalion 314 has shot 294 Jews, Battalion 45 has shot 61 Jews and the Police Squad 113 Jews." Remarkably, the German troops themselves suffered no losses. Another message states that "three Ukrainian and four Russians, presumably parachuters, were transferred to Intelligence; 45 Jews shot." Yet another message reads, "244 Russian soldiers shot, 11 turncoats, two *Flintenweiber* (women in combat) taken prisoner, 84 Jews shot."

28. Husson, "The Extermination of the Ukrainian Jews," 28–30.

29. Lower, *Nazi Empire-Building and the Holocaust in Ukraine*, 1.

30. *Morgenbladet*, July 10, 1941.

31. Rees, *Auschwitz*, 36.

32. Rees, *Auschwitz*, 37.

33. Norwegian News Agency report for *Fritt Folk*, August 19, 1942.

34. *Fritt Folk*, September 1, 1943.

35. Abraham, "Forelebig udö!"

36. Matthäus, "Controlled Escalation," 218–42.

37. Speer, *Fengselsdagbok*, 43.

38. *Germansk Budstikke*, Norwegian edition, booklet 5, 259.

39. Kolsrud, "Kollaborasjon og imperialisme," 243.

40. Kválen, *Dei norske landnám i aust*, 7. Kválen's report was presented on October 22, 1942, and was published as a book in 1944.

41. Kolsrud, "Kollaborasjon og imperialisme," 257.

42. Kolsrud, "Kollaborasjon og imperialisme," 261.

43. Jonas Lie archive, PA 744, National Archives of Norway.

44. Megargee, *War of Annihilation*, 127.

45. Rhodes, *Masters of Death*, 191.

46. Bruland, "NS-styret, frontkjemperne og ugjerningen mot jødene."

47. On May 21, 1941, Jonas Lie was designated the leader of Norges SS by Heinrich Himmler, but since this organization was unsuccessful, it was reorganized the following year.

48. Even Hitler is said to have been impressed by the Russian engineering that created the T-34 tank, a weapon that was superior to what the Germans possessed. Germany didn't manage to produce an answer to these tanks until 1943.

49. In June 1933, the Jewish population in Germany was 503,000. This represented only 0.76 percent of the overall population (Rees, *The Nazis*, 17).

Chapter 7. The Long, Cold Winter

1. *Signal*, Norwegian edition, January 1942. *Signal* was a German magazine that was published in several countries.

2. Petter Westlie, note, December 12, 2003.

3. Herodotus, *The Histories*, 227.

4. Petter Westlie, undated note, probably from between 1993 and 1996.

5. Johansen, *Frontkjemper*, 42.

6. *Hærpilen*, no. 25 (1941).

7. *Hærpilen*, no. 29 (1941).

8. Stridskleiv, "Norske frontkjempere 1941–1945," 1381.

9. Conversation with Petter Westlie, November 28, 2005.

10. *Hærpilen*, January 24, 1942.

11. Petter Westlie to Rolf Westlie, January 27, 1942.

12. Sverresson Sjåstad, "Nordmenn i tysk krigsinnsats," 74.

13. Gjølberg, "Den første jul i et fremmed land."

14. *Nasjonal-Ungdommen: Kampblad for Norges ungdom*, no. 3 (March 1942).

15. *Hirdgjenta: Praktisk handbook for gjente- og småhirden*, published by the National Unification Party Youth Organization, Christmas 1942.

16. Petter Westlie to Rolf Westlie, March 1, 1942.

17. Conversation with Petter Westlie, November 28, 2005.

18. Petter Westlie to Rolf Westlie, March 14, 1942.

19. Conversation with Petter Westlie, August 21, 2005.

Chapter 8. Honor and Allegiance

1. *NS Månedshefte*, no. 7 (1942): 123.

2. Ruge, *Krigens dagbok*, 2:282.

3. Petter Westlie, note, March 1998.

4. *Fritt Folk*, October 3, 1941.

5. *Hærpilen*, no. 25 (1941). The Norwegian Legion, called SS-Freiwilligen-Legion Norwegen in German, was a military division that was established on German initiative in June 1941 to fight on the eastern front. This was after Petter had already enlisted.

6. Ruge, *Krigens dagbok*, 2:282.

7. Japan had ambitions to conquer vast areas of Asia and to establish a powerful empire in alliance with Germany. In 1931, the Japanese occupied Manchuria and set up the puppet state of Manchukuo. From there, they advanced further

into China, conquering Nanjing in 1937, and in 1941, they invaded what was then French Indochina.

8. By declaring war against the United States, Germany opened another front. The British historian and Hitler expert Ian Kershaw has argued that the declaration of war against the US was one of the most self-destructive and ill-considered decisions Hitler made in the war. First, Hitler had gone to war in western Europe, and before that campaign was finished, he opened the front in the east. Then he declared war on the US. Hitler was convinced that the war in Europe would be over before the Americans had a chance to prepare. The problem was that he underestimated the ability of the US to adjust to a war footing, just as he underestimated the Soviet Union's ability to meet his challenges. In addition, by declaring war, Hitler helped President Roosevelt resolve his conflict with Congress about the extent to which the US should be involved in the war. The isolationist voices lost, and the US joined behind Roosevelt in the war against Germany. See Kershaw, *Fateful Choices*, 385–86.

9. Obituary for Reidar Seeberg, "Falt for sitt land," *Fritt Folk*, May 31, 1943. The letter is discussed in the obituary.

10. Petter Westlie to Rolf Westlie, July 10, 1942.

11. Petter Westlie to Rolf Westlie, July 11, 1942.

12. *Fritt Folk*, June 6 and 18, 1942.

13. *Fritt Folk*, May 19, 1942.

14. Frankson and Zetterling, *Slaget om Kursk*, 74.

15. Hamsun, *I Æventyrland*, 114.

16. Eberle and Uhl, *Hitlerboken*, 147.

17. Conversation with Rolf Westlie, January 2007.

18. Conversation with Petter Westlie, April 11, 2006.

19. Beevor, *Stalingrad*, 352.

20. Conversation with Petter Westlie, July 13, 2007.

Chapter 9. Punishment

1. Conversation with Petter Westlie, February 2, 2008.

2. Petter Westlie, undated note.

3. State attorney for cases of treason, indictment, 1297-46 L.

4. Petter Westlie, note, April 10, 2004.

5. Central figures behind the establishment of the Germanic SS Norway were Jonas Lie and Sverre Riisnæs. Many former front soldiers became members.

6. Germanic SS Norway, *SS-Dagen 1943*. This was a propaganda pamphlet that reported on annual events for members.

7. Oppbrudd, 53.

8. Sørensen, *Hitler eller Quis*ling, 81.

9. Rikspropagandaledelsen, *NS Årbok 1944*.

10. Rikspropagandaledelsen, *NS Årbok 1944*.

11. Germanic SS Norway, *SS-Dagen 1943*.

12. Kott, "De tyske politibataljonene i Norge."

13. Lecture from the course for recruits in Germanic SS Norway, articles and lectures, NS Generalsekretariat, PA 759, National Archives of Norway.

14. Petter Westlie to Rolf Westlie, September 12, 1942.

15. *Germaneren*, no 8 (1942): 4.

16. Transcript of receipt from Germanic SS Norway members, Coordination Office, no. 428, 1942, state police, "Jewish action," National Archives of Norway.

17. Karl Marthinsen, chief of state police, report to the head of the security police, November 27, 1942, in author's possession.

18. See "Deportasjonen av de norske jødene," HL-Senteret, October 6, 2011, last updated December 7, 2021, https://www.hlsenteret.no/kunnskapsbasen/folke mord/folkemord-under-nazismen/holocaust/norge/deportasjonen-av-de-norske -jodene.html.

19. Westlie, "Det norske jøderanet"; Westlie, *Oppgjør i skyggen av Holocaust*.

20. Rolf Collin Nielsen, commentary in *NS Årbok 1944*.

21. Letter of support for Petter Westlie as spokesperson, written by several people in Vestre Toten, February 22, 1943, ARK/83, Nasjonal Samling, Vestre Toten Squad, 1940–45, Regional State Archives, Hamar.

22. *Fylkingen*, March 1943.

23. Sivesind, *Motstandskampen på Raufoss 1940–1945*, 139.

24. Walle, *Norsk politi bak piggtråd*, 17.

25. Ringdal, *Mellom barken og veden*, 42.

26. Petter Westlie to unknown (name crossed out), November 2, 1943.

27. *Austrvegr*, March 1944.

28. Conversation with Petter Westlie, February 17, 2008.

29. Petter Westlie, note, April 10, 2005.

30. "Hva skjedde ved Møllergaten 19 natten til 8. mai 1945?," 123–26.

31. Petter Westlie, note, April 10, 2005.

32. Steinsvik, *Frimodige ytringer*.

33. Petter Westlie, undated note.

34. The barracks they lived in are still standing, hidden behind some trees.

35. Vaale, *Dommen til døden*, 185–99.

36. The commission was appointed on June 29, 1945, and assigned the task of evaluating suggestions for the administration of forced labor (Ministry of Justice and Public Security, "Om landssvikoppgjøret," appendix to state notification 17, 1962–63, 393).

37. Interview with Asbjørn Fossen, February 2, 2007.

38. *Akershus Arbeiderblad*, September 1, 1948.

39. Dahl, Hjeltnes, Nøkleby, Ringdal, and Sørensen, *Norsk krigsleksikon 1940–1945*, 389.

40. Conversation with Petter Westlie, February 2, 2008.

41. Ulateig, *Jakten på massemorderne*, 16.

42. Andenæs, *Det vanskelige oppgjøret*, 230.

43. The Bjørkelangen labor camp wasn't closed until March 1955. The twelve remaining prisoners, who had been sentenced to a life term of forced labor, were then transferred to Oslo Prison and Botsfengselet, the former national prison.

Chapter 10. Fear

1. When my father retired, students and instructors at the Academy of Music signed a petition to allow him to continue working.

2. Conversation with Petter Westlie, February 17, 2008.

3. Petter Westlie, undated note.

4. Petter Westlie, note, July 16, 2004. This note was written on an article about Carl I. Hagen's "persecution of Muslims" that was published in *Dagbladet*.

5. Petter Westlie, note, April 4, 2003.

6. Petter Westlie, undated note.

7. Lenz, "Fra matauk til menneskerettigheter," 28. See also Lenz, "Vom Widerstand zum Weltfrieden."

8. Petter Westlie, undated note.

9. Petter Westlie, note, July 2004.

10. Samlerhuset to Petter Westlie, June 18, 2004.

Chapter 11. Black Dogs

1. Evans, *Ukraine*, 65.

2. For example, see Bartov, *Erased*, 31.

3. Zborov is a Polish variant of the name of the Ukrainian town Zboriv. The Norwegian front soldiers knew the town by its Polish name when they passed through Western Ukraine, and that is the name that occurs most often in the sources. Therefore, the author has chosen to use that spelling in this book.

4. Interview with Paltsan Pavlo, Zborov, July 18, 2005.

5. Later, Paltsan found out that the group included not only Jews from Zborov but also from other places in the surrounding areas.

6. Sciolino, "A Priest Methodically Reveals Ukrainian Jews' Fate."

7. See the website for Yahad–In Unum, https://www.yiu.ngo/en.

8. Interview with Patrick Desbois, *Voices on Antisemitism* podcast, https://www.ushmm.org/antisemitism/podcast/voices-on-antisemitism/father-patrick-desbois.

9. Husson, "The Extermination of the Ukrainian Jews," 28–30.

10. The Ukrainian name of Zloczov is Zolotsjiv. The Polish variant is used here, for the same reason as given in note 3 for using Zborov.

11. Strassner, *European Volunteers*, 14.

12. Knopp, *SS*, 190–92.

13. Reinhard Heydrich, "Ereignismeldung Nr. 19 des CSSD von 11.07.1941," Bl. 127, Central Office of the State Justice Administrations for the Investigation of National Socialist Crimes, Ludwigsburg, Germany.

14. Pohl, Nationalsozialistische Judeverfolgung in Ostgalizien, 70.

15. Mayrhofer and Opll, *Juden in der Stadt*, 292.

16. Boll, "Zloczow, July 1941," 70.

17. *Oppbrudd*, 41. Lublin is a city on the Polish side of the border with Ukraine where the soldiers assembled before invading Ukraine.

18. Chef des Generalstabes, July 3, 1941, RH 24–4/38, German Federal Archives, Military Archive.

19. Boll, "Zloczow, July 1941," 73.

20. Boll, "Zloczow, Juli 1941," 911.

21. Friedländer, *The Years of Extermination*, 213. The Organization of Ukrainian Nationalists was established in 1929. Later, the organization was split into two factions: OUN-B, led by Stepan Bandera, and OUN-M, led by Andriy Melnyk. OUN-B was trained by German officers and collaborated with the German troops during and after the invasion. It played a large role in the massacres of Jews. See Boshyk, *Ukraine during World War II*, and Friedländer, *The Years of Extermination*, 223.

22. Boll, "Zloczow, July 1941," 77.

23. Rees, *Auschwitz*, 46.

24. Interview with Katerina Podolyak, July 19, 2005.

25. Telephone interview with Petter Westlie, July 21, 2005.

Chapter 12. The Good, Difficult Discussion

1. This chapter is based on a series of conversations between Petter Westlie and the author that took place from 2005 to 2008.

Epilogue

1. The author has taken excerpts from Ruth Maier's diary and the facts about Maier from a conversation with Jan Erik Vold, September 3, 2005, and from Hofmo, *Jeg glemmer ingen*. The quotations from Ruth Maier's diary, including the ones about my mother, are also found in Vold, *Ruth Maiers dagbok*.

Bibliography

Translator's note: in cases of books translated from English to Norwegian, I have replaced the Norwegian entry with the English original only if I have consulted the original for a quotation in the main text.

Abraham, Ole-Jacob. *"Forelebig udö!": Sovjetiske krigsfangar, norske partisanar og russaren "Nils."* Bergen: Kapabel, 2007.

Ailsby, Christopher. *Images of Barbarossa: The German Invasion of Russia, 1941.* Shepperton: Ian Allan Publishing, 2001.

Ailsby, Christopher. *SS: Hell on the Eastern Front: The Waffen-SS War in Russia, 1941–1945.* Staplehurst: Spellmount, 1998.

Amundsen, Hans. *Trygve Lie: Gutten fra Grorud som ble generalsekretær i FN.* Oslo: Tiden Norsk, 1946.

Andenæs, Johannes. *Det vanskelige oppgjøret.* Oslo: Tanum-Norli, 1979.

Bartov, Omer. *The Eastern Front, 1941–1945: German Troops and the Barbarisation of Warfare.* 2nd ed. New York: Palgrave, 2001.

Bartov, Omer. *Erased: Vanishing Traces of Jewish Galicia in Present-Day Ukraine.* Princeton, NJ: Princeton University Press, 2007.

Bartov, Omer. *Germany's War and the Holocaust: Disputed Histories.* Ithaca, NY: Cornell University Press, 2003.

Bartov, Omer, Atina Grossman, and Mary Nolan, eds. *Crimes of War: Guilt and Denial in the Twentieth Century.* New York: New Press, 2002.

Beevor, Antony. *Stalingrad.* Translated to Norwegian by Bertil Knudsen. Oslo: Spartacus, 2006.

Bellamy, Chris. *Absolute War: Soviet Russia in the Second World War.* London: Macmillan, 2007.

Bishop, Chris. *Hitler's Foreign Divisions: Foreign Volunteers in the Waffen-SS, 1940–1945.* London: Amber Books, 2005.

Boll, Bernd. "Zloczow, Juli 1941: Die Wehrmacht und der Beginn des Holocaust in Galizien." *Zeitschrift für Geschichtswissenschaft* 10 (2002): 899–917.

Boll, Bernd. "Zloczow, July 1941: The Wehrmacht and the Beginning of the Holocaust in Galicia." In *Crimes of War: Guilt and Denial in the Twentieth Century*, edited by Omer Bartov, Atina Grossman, and Mary Nolan, 61–99. New York: New Press, 2002.

Bonn, Keith. *Slaughterhouse: The Handbook of the Eastern Front*. Bedford, PA: Aberjona, 2005.

Boshyk, Yury, ed. *Ukraine during World War II: History and Its Aftermath*. Edmonton: Canadian Institute of Ukrainian Studies, University of Alberta, 1986.

Braithwaite, Rodric. *Moskva 1941*. Translated by Carsten Carlsen. Oslo: Cappelen Damm, 2007.

Brevig, Hans Olaf, and Ivo de Figueiredo. *Den norske fascismen: Nasjonal Samling, 1933–1940*. Oslo: Pax, 2002.

Bruland, Bjarte. *Holocaust i Norge: Registrering, deportasjon, tilintetgjørelse*. Oslo: Dreyer, 2017.

Bruland, Bjarte. "NS-styret, frontkjemperne og ugjerningen mot jødene." *Aftenposten*, December 4, 2004.

Bundgård Christen, Claes, Niels Bo Paulsen, and Peter Scharff Smith. *Dagbog fra Østfronten: En dansker i Waffen-SS 1941–1944*. Copenhagen: Aschehoug, 2005.

Bundgård Christen, Claes, Niels Bo Paulsen, and Peter Scharff Smith. *Under hagekors og Dannebrog. Danskere i Waffen-SS 1940–1945*. Copenhagen: Aschehoug, 1998.

Butler, Rupert. *SS-Wiking: The History of the Fifth SS Division*. London: Amber Books, 2002.

Dahl, Hans Fredrik. *Hallo—Hallo! Kringkastingen i Norge 1920–1940*. Oslo: Cappelen, 1999.

Dahl, Hans Fredrik, Bernt Hagtvedt, and Guri Hjeltnes. *Den norske nasjonalsosialismen*. Oslo: Pax, 1982.

Dahl, Hans Fredrik, Guri Hjeltnes, Berit Nøkleby, Nils Johan Ringdal, and Øystein Sørensen, eds. *Norsk krigsleksikon 1940–1945*. Oslo: Cappelen, 1995.

Davidsen, Leif, and Karsten Lindhardt. *Østfronten: Danskere i krig*. Copenhagen: Høst & Søn, 1999.

Eberle, Henrik, and Matthias Uhl, eds. *Hitlerboken: Stalins hemmelige dokument*. Oslo: Aschehoug, 2007.

Emberland, Terje, and Matthew Kott. *Himmlers Norge: Nordmenn i det storgermanske prosjekt*. Oslo: Aschehoug, 2012.

Emberland, Terje, and Bernt Rougthvedt. *Det ariske idol: Forfatteren, eventyreren og nazisten Per Imerslund*. Oslo: Aschehoug, 2004.

Evans, Andrew. *Ukraine: The Bradt Travel Guide*. Chesham, UK: Bradt, 2007.

Fest, Joachim. *Hitler*. Oslo: Gyldendal, 1973.

Fjørtoft, Kjell. *De som tapte krigen*. Oslo: Gyldendal, 1995.

Fjørtoft, Kjell. *Veien til Østfronten: Krigens mange ansikter*. Oslo: Gyldendal, 1993.

Förster, Jürgen. "Die weltanschauliche Erzeihung von SS, Polizei und Waffen-SS im Rahmen der 'Endlösung.'" In *Ausbildungsziel Judenmord?*, edited by Jürgen Matthäus, Konrad Kweit, Jürgen Förster, and Richard Breitman, 98–99. Frankfurt: Fischer, 2003.

Frankson, Anders, and Miklas Zetterling. *Slaget om Kursk: Historiens største panserslag*. Oslo: Spartacus, 2006.

Friedländer, Saul. *The Years of Extermination: Nazi Germany and the Jews, 1939–1945*. New York: HarperCollins, 2008.

Fure, Odd-Bjørn. "Norsk okkupasjonshistorie: Konsensus, berøringsangst, og tabuisering." In *I krigens kjølvann: Nye sider ved norsk krigshistorie og etterkrigstid*, edited by Stein Ugelvik Larsen, 31–46. Oslo: Universitetsforlaget, 1999.

Fure, Odd-Bjørn, and Tom B. Jensen. *Mellomkrigstid 1920–1940*. Oslo: Universitetsforlaget, 1996.

Glantz, David M. *Before Stalingrad: Barbarossa—Hitler's Invasion of Russia 1941*. Stroud: Tempus, 2003.

Gjølberg, Thoralf. "Den første jul i et fremmed land." *Austvegr*, no. 1 (1942).

Grimnes, Ole Kristian. *Norge under andre verdenskrig, 1939–1945*. Oslo: Aschehoug, 2018.

Grossman, Vasily. *A Writer at War: A Soviet Journalist with the Red Army, 1941–1945*. Edited and translated by Antony Beevor and Luba Vinogradova. London: Harvill Press, 2005.

Gyllenhaal, Lars, and Lennart Westberg. *Svenskar i krig: 1914–1945*. Lund: Historiska Media, 2006.

Hamsun, Knut. *I Æventyrland: Oplevet og drømt i Kaukasien*. 1903. Reprint, Oslo: Gyldendal, 2000.

Hansen, Tommy. "NS på Gjøvik 1933–1940." Sogn og Fjordane University College, spring 1999.

Heer, Hannes. *"Hitler war's": Die Befreiung der Deutschen von ihrer Vergangenheit*. Berlin: Aufbau, 2008.

Heer, Hannes. *Vom Verschwinden der Täter: Der Vernichtungskrieg fand statt, aber keiner war dabei*. Berlin: Aufbau, 2005.

Hegtun, Halfdan. *Rundt fabrikken*. Oslo: Aschehoug, 1984.

Hem, Erlend, and Per E. Børdahl. "En nød som ord ikke kan beskrive—leger på flukt til Norge 1939–40." *Tidsskrift for Den norske Lægeforening* 30, no. 10 (2001): 3568–73.

Herodotus. *The Histories*. Translated by A. D. Godley. Cambridge, MA: Harvard University Press, 1920.

Hillberg, Raul. *The Destruction of the European Jews*. New York: Holmes and Meier, 1985.

Hitler, Adolf. *Mein Kampf*. Boston: Houghton Mifflin, 1939.

Hofmo, Gunvor. *Jeg glemmer ingen*. Oslo: Gyldendal, 1999.

Holmen, Rolf. *Kaare: Historien om en totning og mennesker han møtte*. Gjøvik: Alfa, 2005.

Holmen, Rolf. "Raufoss og andre verdenskrig." In *Totn årbok*, 2000–2001, 155. Oppland: Stiftelsen Toten Økomuseum og historielag.

Holmen, Rolf, and Thor Wang. *Vår kamp for rettferd og framgang: Raufoss Jern & Metall 1905–2005*. Gjøvik: Alfa, 2005.

Husson, Edouard. "The Extermination of the Ukrainian Jews." In *The Mass Shooting of Jews in Ukraine, 1941–1944: The Holocaust by Bullets*, 28–30. Paris: Yahad–In Unum, Fondation pour la Mémoire de la Shoah, 2007.

"Hva skjedde ved Møllergaten 19 natten til 8. mai 1945?" In *Norsk Politihistorisk Selskaps årsskrift*, 123–25. Oslo: Norsk Politihistorisk Selskaps, 2000.

Johansen, Per R. *Frontkjemper*. Oslo: Aschehoug, 1992.

Jordbruen, Rolf Ivar. *Helvete på jord: En frontkjempers historie*. Oslo: Spartacus, 2006.

Kabanchik, I. B. *Places of Dolour: Lvov Region*. Lvov: Lvov Holocaust Center, 2003.

Kern, Erich. *Kampf in der Ukraine 1941–44*. Göttingen: Presse-Verlag, 1964.

Kershaw, Ian. *Fateful Choices: Ten Decisions That Changed the World*. London: Allen Lane, 2007.

Kirkebæk, Mikkel. *Schalburg—en patriotisk landsforræder*. Copenhagen: Gyldendal, 2008.

Knopp, Guido. *SS: Historien om nazistenes leiemordere*. Translated into Norwegian by Eli Aakre. Oslo: Historie & Kultur, 2007.

Kolloen, Ingar Sletten. *Hamsun: Svermeren*. Oslo: Gyldendal, 2003.

Kolsrud, Ole. "Kollaborasjon og imperialism: Quisling-regjeringens 'Austveg'-drøm 1941–1944." *Historisk tidsskrift* 67, no. 3 (1988): 241–70.

Kosyk, Wolodymyr. *The Third Reich and Ukraine*. Frankfurt am Main: Peter Lang, 1993.

Kott, Matthew. "De tyske politibataljonene i Norge." Lecture, August 8, 2008, Research Seminar on Norwegians in the Waffen-SS, Kongsvinger, Norway.

Kválen, Eivind. *Dei norske landnám i aust*. Oslo: Viking, 1944.

Landau, Felix. "Once Again I Get to Play General to the Jews." In *The Good Old Days: The Holocaust as Seen by Its Perpetrators and Bystanders*, edited by Ernst

Klee, Willy Dressen, and Volker Riess, 87–106. Old Saybrook, CT: Konecky and Konecky, 1991.

Larsen, Stein Ugelvik, ed. *I krigens kjølvann: Nye sider ved norsk krigshistorie og etterkrigstid.* Oslo: Universitetsforlaget, 1999.

Larsen, Stein Ugelvik. "The Social Foundation of Norwegian Fascism, 1933–1945: An Analysis of Membership Data." In *Who Were the Fascists? Social Roots of European Fascism*, edited by Stein Ugelvik Larsen, Bernt Hagtvet, and Jan Petter Myklebust, 595–620. Oslo: Universitetsforlaget, 1980.

Larsen, Stein Ugelvik, Bernt Hagtvet, and Jan Petter Myklebust, eds. *Who Were the Fascists? Social Roots of European Fascism.* Oslo: Universitetsforlaget, 1980.

Lenz, Claudia. "Fra matauk til menneskerettigheter: Fortelling og fortolkning av kriseminner i norske familier gjennom tre generasjoner." *Fortid*, no. 2 (2007): 22–29.

Lenz, Claudia. "Vom Widerstand zum Weltfrieden." In *Der Krieg der Erinnerung: Holocaust, Kollaboration und Widerstand im europäischen Gedächtnis*, edited by Harald Welzer, 41–76. Frankfurt am Main: Fischer, 2007.

Lie, Jonas. *Over Balkans syv blåner.* Oslo: Blix, 1942.

Longerich, Peter. *Dette viste vi ikke noe om: Tyskerne og jødeforfølgelsene 1933–1945.* Oslo: Historie & Kultur, 2007.

Løvlie, Arne. "Norske våpen i tyske hender." *Forsvarsmuseets Småskrift* 40 (2004): 135.

Lower, Wendy. *Nazi Empire-Building and the Holocaust in Ukraine.* Chapel Hill: University of North Carolina Press, 2005.

Lucas, James. *War on the Eastern Front: The German Soldier in Russia, 1941–1945.* London: Greenhill Books, 1991.

Magocsi, Paul Robert. *A History of Ukraine.* Toronto: University of Toronto Press, 1996.

Malde, Per. *Kall det vrede.* Oslo: Tiden Norsk, 1991.

Matthäus, Jürgen, ed. *Ausbildungsziel Judenmord? "Weltanschauliche Erziehung" von SS, Polizei und Waffen-SS im Rahmen der "Endlösung."* Frankfurt am Main: Fischer, 2003.

Matthäus, Jürgen. "Controlled Escalation: Himmler's Men in the Summer of 1941 and the Holocaust in the Occupied Soviet Territories." *Holocaust and Genocide Studies* 21, no. 2, (2007): 218–42.

Mawdsley, Evan. *Thunder in the East: The Nazi-Soviet War 1941–1945.* London: Hodder Education, 2005.

Mayrhofer, Fritz, and Ferdinand Opll. *Juden in der Stadt: Beiträge zur Geschichte der Städte Mitteleuropas.* Vol. 15. Linz: Österreichisches Arbeitskreises für Stadtgeschichtsforschung, 1999.

McCarthy, Peter, and Mike Syron. *Panzerkrieg: A History of the German Tank Division in World War II*. London: Robinson, 2003.

Megargee, Geoffrey P. *War of Annihilation: Combat and Genocide on the Eastern Front*. Lanham, MD: Rowan and Littlefield, 2007.

Mendelsohn, Oskar. *Jødenes historie i Norge gjennom 300 år 1940*. 2 vols. Oslo: Universitetsforlaget, 1986.

Metelmann, Henry. *Through Hell for Hitler: A Dramatic First-Hand Account of Fighting on the Eastern Front with the Wehrmacht*. Havertown, PA: Casemate, 2005.

Murphy, David E. *What Stalin Knew*. New Haven, CT: Yale University Press, 2005.

Myklebust, Jan Petter, and Bernt Hagtvet. "Regional Contrasts in the Membership Base of the Nasjonal Samling." In *Who Were the Fascists? Social Roots of European Fascism*, edited by Stein Ugelvik Larsen, Bernt Hagtvet, and Jan Petter Myklebust, 621–50. Oslo: Universitetsforlaget, 1980.

Neumann, Peter. *Dødens drabanter*. Oslo: Stensballe, 1959.

Nøkleby, Berit. *Hitlers Norge: Okkupasjonsmakten, 1940–1945*. Oslo: Cappelen Damm, 2016.

"Norske fotballgutter gjorde Hitler rasende." In *"Jeg så det hende": Øyenvitner til norsk historie 1900–1955*, edited by Kjell Pihlstrøm and Harald Queseth, 87–90. Oslo: Tiden Norsk, 1989.

Oppbrudd: Brever fra germanske krigsfrivillige. Oslo: Kamban, 1943.

Pihlstrøm, Kjell, and Harald Queseth. *"Jeg så det hende": Øyenvitner til norsk historie 1900–1955*. Oslo: Tiden Norsk, 1989.

Pohl, Dieter. *Nationalsozialistische Judeverfolgung in Ostgalizien, 1941–1944*. Munich: Oldenbourg, 1997.

Pryser, Tore. *Klassen og nasjonen: Arbeiderbevegelsens historie i Norge*. Oslo: Tiden Norsk, 1988.

Quisling, Vidkun. *Kampen mellom arier og jødemakt*. Oslo: Nasjonal Samlings Rikstrykkeri, 1941.

Quisling, Vidkun. *Quisling har sagt: For Norges frihet og selvstendighet*. Oslo: Stenersen, 1941.

Rees, Laurence. *Auschwitz: A New History*. New York: Public Affairs, 2005.

Rees, Laurence. *The Nazis: A Warning from History*. London: BBC Books, 2005.

Rhodes, Richard. *Masters of Death: The SS-Einsatzgruppen and the Invention of the Holocaust*. New York: Knopf, 2002.

Rikmenspoel, Marc J. *Waffen-SS Encyclopedia*. Bedford, PA: Aberjona, 2004.

Ringdal, Nils Johan. *Mellom barken og veden*. Oslo: Aschehoug, 1987.

Ripley, Tim. *Hitler's Praetorians: The History of the Waffen-SS, 1925–1945.* Staple-hurst: Spellmont, 2004.

Ruge, Otto. *Krigens dagbok: Annen verdenskrig i tekst og billeder.* 3 vols. Oslo: Halvorsen & Larsen, 1946–47.

Sæther, Vegard. *"En av oss"—Norske frontkjempere i krig og fred.* Oslo: Cappelen Damm, 2010.

Schaap, Jeremy. *Triumph: The Untold Story of Jesse Owens and Hitler's Olympics.* Boston: Houghton Mifflin, 2007.

Schön, Bosse. *Svenskarna som stred för Hitler.* Stockholm: Bokforlaget DN, 1999.

Sciolino, Elaine. "A Priest Methodically Reveals Ukrainian Jews' Fate." *New York Times,* October 6, 2007.

Seiffert, Rachel. *Mørkerommet.* Oslo: Cappelen Damm, 2006.

Simon, Hermann, Irene Stratenwerth, and Ronald Hinrichs. *Lemberg: Eine Reise nach Europa.* Berlin: Christoph Links, 2007.

Sivesind, Oskar. *Motstandskampen på Raufoss 1940–45.* Self-published, 1995.

Skjønsfjell, Jan. "Frontkjempere fra Troms: Bakgrunn og motivasjon." Master's thesis, University of Tromsø, 2005.

Sørensen, Øystein. *Hitler eller Quisling: Ideologiske brytninger i Nasjonal Samling 1940–1945.* Oslo: Cappelen, 1989.

Sørlie, Sigurd. *Solkors eller hakekors: Nordmenn i Waffen-SS, 1941–1945.* Oslo: Dreyer, 2015.

Sørlie, Sigurd, Matthew Kott, and Terje Emberland. "I krig for Hitler: Nordmenn i tysk rikstjeneste." *Fortid,* no. 2 (2007): 55–60.

Speer, Albert. *Erindringer.* Oslo: Gyldendal, 2005.

Speer, Albert. *Fengselsdagbok.* Oslo: Gyldendal, 1976.

Steinsvik, Marta. *Frimodige ytringer.* Self-published, 1946.

Stenseth, Bodil. *Sonja: Kvinne på is.* Oslo: Pax, 2002.

Strassner, Peter. *European Volunteers: The 5. SS Panzer-Division Wiking.* Winnipeg: J. J. Fedorowicz, 1998.

Stridskleiv, Inger Cecilie. "Norske frontkjempere 1941–1945, 50 år senere: Erfaringer, belastning, helsemessige og sosiale forhold." *Tidsskrift for Den norske Lægeforen-ing* 115, no. 11 (1995): 1379–84.

Subtelny, Orest. "The Soviet Occupation of Western Ukraine, 1939–41: An Over-view." In *Ukraine during World War II: History and Its Aftermath: A Symposium,* edited by Roman Waschuk, 5–14. Toronto: University of Toronto Press, 1986.

Subtelny, Orest. *Ukraine: A History.* Toronto: University of Toronto Press, 2000.

Sverresson Sjåstad, Gunnar. "Nordmenn i tysk krigsinnsats: En kvantitativ under-søkelse av frontkjempere under den andre verdenskrig." Master's thesis, Univer-sity of Bergen, 2006.

Ulateig, Egil. *Jakten på massemorderne: En dokumentarbok.* Lesja: Forlaget Reportasje, 2006.Ulateig, Egil, and Geir Brenden. *Nordmenn på Østfronten.* Forlaget Reportasje, 2005.

Vaale, Lars-Erik. *Dommen til døden: Dødsstraffen i Norge 1945–1950.* Oslo: Pax, 2004.

Vetlesen, Arne Johan. *Evil and Human Agency: Understanding Collective Evildoing.* Cambridge: Cambridge University Press, 2005.

Vold, Jan Erik, ed. *Ruth Maiers dagbok: En jødisk flyktning i Norge.* Oslo: Gyldendal, 2007.

Waage, Peter Normann. *Når kulturer kolliderer.* Oslo: Aventura, 1989.

Walle, Olaf R. *Norsk politi bak piggtråd: Stutthofspolitiets historie 1943–1945.* Tvedestrand: Naper Boktrykkeri, 1946.

Wang, Thor. *RA i skuddlinja.* Raufoss: Thor Wang, 1996.

Welzer, Harald, ed. *Der Krieg der Erinnerung: Holocaust, Kollaboration und Widerstand im europäischen Gedächtnis.* Frankfurt am Main: Fischer, 2007.

Westlie, Bjørn. "Det norske jøderanet," *Dagens Næringsliv,* May 27, 1995, 10–13.

Westlie, Bjørn. *Det norske jødehatet: Propaganda og presse under okkupasjonen.* Oslo: Res Publica, 2019.

Westlie, Bjørn. *Oppgjør i skyggen av Holocaust.* Oslo: Aschehoug, 2002.

Wette, Wolfram. *The Wehrmacht: History, Myth, and Reality.* Cambridge, MA: Harvard University Press, 2006.

Wibe, Harald. "Mennesker og jøder." *Baunen,* August 9, 1941.

Zamoyski, Adam. *1812: Napoleons russiske tragedie.* Oslo: Schibsted, 2007.

Zantrop, Susanne. *Colonial Fantasies: Family and Nation in Precolonial Germany, 1770–1870.* Durham, NC: Duke University Press, 1997.